St Lucia

WORLD BIBLIOGRAPHICAL SERIES

General Editors:
Robert G. Neville (Executive Editor)
John J. Horton

Robert A. Myers   Hans H. Wellisch
Ian Wallace   Ralph Lee Woodward, Jr.

John J. Horton is Deputy Librarian of the University of Bradford and was formerly Chairman of its Academic Board of Studies in Social Sciences. He has maintained a longstanding interest in the discipline of area studies and its associated bibliographical problems, with special reference to European Studies. In particular he has published in the field of Icelandic and of Yugoslav studies, including the two relevant volumes in the World Bibliographical Series.

Robert A. Myers is Associate Professor of Anthropology in the Division of Social Sciences and Director of Study Abroad Programs at Alfred University, Alfred, New York. He has studied post-colonial island nations of the Caribbean and has spent two years in Nigeria on a Fulbright Lectureship. His interests include international public health, historical anthropology and developing societies. In addition to *Amerindians of the Lesser Antilles: a bibliography* (1981), *A Resource Guide to Dominica, 1493-1986* (1987) and numerous articles, he has compiled the World Bibliographical Series volumes on *Dominica* (1987), *Nigeria* (1989) and *Ghana* (1991).

Ian Wallace is Professor of German at the University of Bath. A graduate of Oxford in French and German, he also studied in Tübingen, Heidelberg and Lausanne before taking teaching posts at universities in the USA, Scotland and England. He specializes in contemporary German affairs, especially literature and culture, on which he has published numerous articles and books. In 1979 he founded the journal *GDR Monitor*, which he continues to edit under its new title *German Monitor*.

Hans H. Wellisch is Professor emeritus at the College of Library and Information Services, University of Maryland. He was President of the American Society of Indexers and was a member of the International Federation for Documentation. He is the author of numerous articles and several books on indexing and abstracting, and has published *The Conversion of Scripts and Indexing and Abstracting: an International Bibliography*, and *Indexing from A to Z*. He also contributes frequently to *Journal of the American Society for Information Science*, *The Indexer* and other professional journals.

Ralph Lee Woodward, Jr. is Professor of History at Tulane University, New Orleans. He is the author of *Central America, a Nation Divided*, 2nd ed. (1985), as well as several monographs and more than seventy scholarly articles on modern Latin America. He has also compiled volumes in the World Bibliographical Series on *Belize* (1980), *El Salvador* (1988), *Guatemala* (Rev. Ed.) (1992) and *Nicaragua* (Rev. Ed.) (1994). Dr. Woodward edited the Central American section of the *Research Guide to Central America and the Caribbean* (1985) and is currently associate editor of Scribner's *Encyclopedia of Latin American History*.

VOLUME 185

St Lucia

Janet Henshall Momsen

Compiler

CLIO PRESS

OXFORD, ENGLAND · SANTA BARBARA, CALIFORNIA
DENVER, COLORADO

© Copyright 1996 by ABC-CLIO Ltd.

British Library Cataloguing in Publication Data

St Lucia – (World Bibliographical Series;
Vol. 185)
I. Momsen, Janet Henshall. II. Series
016.972 9843

ISBN 1–85109–136–X

ABC-CLIO Ltd.,
Old Clarendon Ironworks,
35A Great Clarendon Street,
Oxford OX2 6AT, England.

—————

ABC-CLIO Inc.,
130 Cremona Drive,
Santa Barbara,
CA 93116, USA.

Designed by Bernard Crossland.
Typeset by Columns Design and Production Services Ltd., Reading, England.
Printed and bound in Great Britain by Bookcraft (Bath) Ltd., Midsomer Norton.

THE WORLD BIBLIOGRAPHICAL SERIES

This series, which is principally designed for the English speaker, will eventually cover every country (and many of the world's principal regions), each in a separate volume comprising annotated entries on works dealing with its history, geography, economy and politics; and with its people, their culture, customs, religion and social organization. Attention will also be paid to current living conditions – housing, education, newspapers, clothing, etc. – that are all too often ignored in standard bibliographies; and to those particular aspects relevant to individual countries. Each volume seeks to achieve, by use of careful selectivity and critical assessment of the literature, an expression of the country and an appreciation of its nature and national aspirations, to guide the reader towards an understanding of its importance. The keynote of the series is to provide, in a uniform format, an interpretation of each country that will express its culture, its place in the world, and the qualities and background that make it unique. The views expressed in individual volumes, however, are not necessarily those of the publisher.

VOLUMES IN THE SERIES

*For my mother, Rick
and Valerie*

Contents

Contents

Introduction

St Lucia, often called the Helen of the West Indies, was considered by Charles Kingsley to be the most beautiful island in the Lesser Antilles. The second largest of the Leeward and Windward Islands, it is situated on the island arc of the eastern Caribbean, between the French Département of Martinique and the British Commonwealth island of St Vincent, and 110 miles north-west of Barbados. Located at approximately Latitude 14°N and Longitude 61°W, the island is roughly forty-three kilometres long and twenty-two kilometres wide, with a total area of 617.5 square kilometres, just a little bigger than the Isle of Man. St Lucia's proximity to both British and French settlements meant that for a long period after its discovery the island was the constant focus of colonial disputes, changing hands between the European powers fourteen times. Two centuries of such turbulence fostered the creation of a unique Anglo-French culture and inhibited the development of plantation agriculture so preserving much of the indigenous flora and fauna.

The environment

The island is volcanic in origin, with a rugged interior of forest-clad hills intersected by valleys of banana and coconut plantations. The highest point is Morne Gimie, which climbs to a height of 944 metres, but the most spectacular peaks, the Gros Piton (786 metres) and the Petit Piton (738 metres), are precipitous volcanic plugs which rise steeply up out of the sea just south of the town of Soufrière. A few miles inland is a 'drive-in' volcano, which is entered through a break in the edge of a caldera, thought to have collapsed some 40,000 years ago. The bubbling mineral-rich grey mud found here and active sulphur springs in which the water may reach temperatures of 121°C draw many tourists to the area, which has also attracted considerable geothermal research since 1974.

Introduction

Drowned volcanic craters have provided St Lucia with two magnificent harbours. Castries harbour is probably the best in the West Indies and was the reason for St Lucia's importance in colonial times as a naval base and a coaling station. It now attracts cruise ships and yachts. Marigot Bay is much smaller but is said to have enabled the British Navy to lie hidden there during the eighteenth-century wars with France, as well as supplying the location for the film *Dr Doolittle*.

Evidence of uplift can be seen in the layers of Pleistocene coral limestone which are visible some thirty to fifty metres up in the perpendicular cliffs on the west coast near Malgrétout. A relatively recent uplift of fifteen to thirty metres at both ends of the island is thought to explain the marine terrace deposits around Vieux Fort in the south and the raised beaches of the Gros Islet area in the north of the island. The northern and western parts of the island are the oldest with the most mature relief and broad alluvial valleys, such as those of the Roseau and Cul-de-Sac rivers. The large fan-shaped glacis slopes of the south-west are considered to be the youngest part of the island. The main underlying rock types are basalts, andesites and dacites but these are often overlain by relatively recent ash deposits so that many of St Lucia's soils are developed from a combination of different lithological parent materials. Roadcuts reveal soil profiles with various layers of volcanic ash and coarser rock deposits. Many of the soils of St Lucia's interior are very susceptible to erosion and the steep topography and heavy rainfall exacerbate this danger. Rock and mud slides sometimes occur and in 1938 avalanches of this nature resulted in a number of deaths. Unusually for a volcanic island, St Lucia has magnificent white sandy beaches which provide an important resource base for the tourism industry.

The climate in the island is tropical with little diurnal or annual temperature variation. Winter temperatures range from 18°C (65°F) to 29°C (85°F) and summer temperatures from 24°C (75°F) to 35°C (95°F) with the heat mitigated by the north-east trade winds which freshen during the dry season. Rainfall has a concentric pattern, being lowest in the north and south of the island and highest on Morne Gimie; annual rainfall totals range between 160cm and 360cm. In the winter months rain takes the form of short showers, resulting from cold fronts from the North American continent. In summer rainfall is heavier and is both convectional and related to movement of the inter-tropical convergence zone. The driest months are January to April and the wettest May to September. Hurricanes and tropical storms usually occur between July and November and in the last fifteen years St Lucia has suffered from several major storms and hurricanes which have caused considerable damage to the island's main export crop, bananas. In 1980 Hurricane Allen resulted in loss of life and the total destruction of the banana fields while a fierce tropical storm in 1994 devastated two-thirds of the banana crop.

During colonial times timber was a major export for St Lucia and it was only in 1939 that the island, for the first time, imported more wood than it exported. Moreover, the rapid expansion of the banana industry in the 1960s led to widespread forest clearance. This deforestation has resulted in increased susceptibility to soil erosion, lower rainfall and reduced or even intermittent stream flow. In addition, the expansion of farming into the upper reaches of streams has extended the area contaminated with bilharzia (schistosomiasis), as the disease is dependent on the freshwater snail, *Biomphalaria Glabrata*, as an intermediate host. Much of the remaining rainforest along the spine of the island is now protected, mainly for water supply but also for wildlife, and on the highest slopes of Morne Gimie there is a small area of elfin woodland. The northern and southern tips of the island have zerophytic vegetation of thorn scrub and cacti.

St Lucia has several endemic species of birds and reptiles and has long had one of the most active conservation movements in the region. The first Wild Bird Protection Ordinance was passed in 1885 but was not effectively implemented. Consequently, by 1950 the St Lucia Parrot had become the rarest of the Caribbean amazons. The main nesting sites of this national bird, the multicoloured, brilliantly plumaged *Amazona versicolor*, are now protected and a programme instituted in 1978 has allowed the number of parrots to rise from just 150 in 1978 to over 400 today despite the depredations of recent hurricanes. Other endemic species to the island are the black finch, the oriole and the nightjar, although the native Semper's warbler (*Leucopeza semperi*) is now probably extinct. In addition, a major south-east coast conservation programme is being co-ordinated by the Eastern Caribbean Natural Areas Management Programme (ECNAMP) and off the southern tip of St Lucia, the Maria Islands, home to four endemic reptiles, have been made a protected area under the management of the St Lucia National Trust. In the central east coast area, Fregate Island Nature Reserve, on the northern side of Praslin Bay, was handed over to the National Trust in 1989. The Reserve has nesting sites for the frigate bird, and was the location of an Amerindian lookout and of a battle between the English and the Brigands. Savannes Bay Nature Reserve, a little further south, is protected for its mangroves, sea moss, conch and sea eggs and recently excavated archaeological sites.

Introduction

History

Some St Lucians claim that their island was discovered by Columbus in 1502 on St Lucy's day, the 13 December and now a national holiday, but evidence from Columbus' log supports the view that he missed the island and was not even in the area on St Lucy's day. Neither the date of discovery nor the discoverer are definitively known but a Vatican globe of 1520 marks the island as Santa Lucia, suggesting that it was at least claimed by Spain by that date. In 1605, the *Orange Blossom*, with sixty-seven Englishmen on board, en route to Guiana, visited St Lucia after calling at Barbados. It is also thought a Dutch expedition may have discovered the island earlier and built a fort there.

At the time of first contact the island was occupied by Caribs and many of their settlement sites have since been discovered, especially on the windward coast. These sites have yielded both Carib and Arawak artefacts such as petroglyphs, pottery and stone tools. The Amerindians called their island Iouanalao which may have meant 'the place where the iguana is found'. The name was later changed to Hwanarau which then evolved to Hewanorra, the name now given to the island's main airport. The Caribs fiercely resisted the European 'invasion' of their island. The first recorded settlement was made by English colonists from Bermuda and St Kitts in 1638, under the command of a Captain Judlee, but its existence was very brief.

In 1642 the King of France claimed sovereignty over the island, ceding it to the French West India Company, which in 1650 sold it, with Grenada and Martinique, to MM Houel and Du Parquet for £1,660 sterling. Forty settlers were sent to St Lucia. Their leader was M. Rousselan, who married a Carib woman, thereby securing friendly relations between the French and the Caribs. Rousselan introduced the cultivation of cotton, tobacco and ginger to the island. On his death in 1654, however, the Caribs made repeated attempts to expel the French settlers and three governors were killed before a treaty was signed in 1660 (Treaty of St Christopher's) promising the Caribs freedom from interference in Dominica and St Vincent on condition they kept the peace elsewhere. From 1660 the British began to renew their claim to the island and fighting for possession began in earnest. As early as 1652 St Lucia was seen as an outlet for the surplus population of Barbados, a view which continued into the twentieth century. In 1664 Lord Willoughby sent some 1,500 Barbadians to the island defraying their expenses with a 4.5 per cent duty levied on exports which was not finally abolished until 1838. The French were overpowered but because of sickness, famine and disputes with the

Caribs which reduced the number of settlers to a mere eighty-nine, the English evacuated the island in 1666. A new French West India company took over and, in 1667, St Lucia once again became a French colony under the Peace of Breda. In 1718 Marshal d'Estrées was granted St Lucia. He sent out an expedition to colonize the island but the English remonstrated and no effective settlement was achieved. Four years later the island was granted by King George I to the Duke of Montagu who also sent out colonists. An ineffectual attempt was made by Captain Uring to settle in St Lucia but this was prevented by a French force from Martinique. It was agreed that both nations should evacuate the island, only visiting for the purpose of obtaining wood and water, until such time as a political decision could be made about ownership. In 1748 the island was declared to be neutral by the Treaty of Aix-la-Chapelle although this did not deter the French from continuing their colonization. The island capitulated to the forces of Admiral Rodney and General Monckton in 1762 but was restored to France in the following year by the Treaty of Paris.

In 1725 a few French planters from Martinique were induced to settle in St Lucia; they established coffee and cocoa estates there but the lack of security of tenure did not encourage an expansion of their activities. In 1745 the first official grant of land was made by Governor de Longueville and after 1763 many French settlers fled English rule in Grenada and St Vincent and settled in St Lucia, bringing with them capital and slaves. This influx marked the real beginning of the plantation economy on the island and the first sugar was produced in 1765 near Vieux Fort. By 1780 there were thirty producing sugar estates and another twenty were being planted when a hurricane destroyed most of the estates and sugar mills. The French government, finding that the resources of the island could not support a separate administration under a Governor-General as established in 1764, re-annexed it to Martinique in 1768. At this time the population of the island was estimated at 12,794 but by 1772 it had risen to 15,446, made up of 2,018 whites, 633 coloured and 12,795 blacks.

When war broke out with France in 1778, Admiral Rodney persuaded the British Government of the importance of taking St Lucia which he regarded as an ideal naval base, and troops were landed at Grand Cul-de-Sac Bay. They were able to beat off the forces of the Comte d'Estaing and until the end of the war the island remained British in spite of an attempt by the French to recapture it in 1781. Rodney established a lookout on Pigeon Island from where he was able to keep an eye on the movement of the French fleet stationed in Martinique. By April 1782, island after island had fallen into French hands and the French forces were preparing for an assault on

Jamaica. Admiral Rodney and the English fleet set sail from Gros Islet Bay and engaged the French fleet, under the command of the Comte de Grasse, in battle off the coast of Dominica. Although the French forces were the larger, Rodney broke the enemy's line of battle and inflicted a decisive defeat, in which 261 English sailors were killed and 837 wounded while no fewer than 14,000 French were accounted for as dead or wounded. This battle secured England's West Indian colonies, yet in the Treaty of Versailles of 1783 St Lucia was restored to the French.

Many planters held land in both Martinique and St Lucia and it is believed that Josephine Tascher de la Pagerie, who later became the Empress Josephine Bonaparte, was born on St Lucia at Paix Bouche just north of Castries in 1764, although her family left St Lucia in 1771 for Martinique. About the same time, in 1770, Jean Baptiste Bideau, was born in the eastern village of Desruisseaux. He became a seaman, saved the life of Simón Bolivar and died in 1817 fighting for the independence of Venezuela. He now has a square in Castries named after him.

Under the governorship of the Baron de Laborie, the settlement of the island was carefully planned and rapid development took place, with foreign settlers allowed equal rights even when their countries were at war with France. The streets of Castries were paved and roads were built and improved throughout the island. The Baron had baths constructed at the mineral springs near Soufrière although they were destroyed in the Brigands War a few years later. He also encouraged agriculture, especially spice cultivation, for which he had plants imported from Cayenne. By the time the Baron de Laborie died in 1789 the population of the island had risen to 21,778 (2,198 white people, 1,588 coloured and 17,992 blacks).

A survey of the island carried out by M. Lefort de Latour in 1787 recorded land use and land ownership. Much of the land was found to be abandoned because of the turmoil of war and the severe hurricane of 1780 and all but two of the landowners depicted on the 1787 map have French names. At this time, since communication was dependent on sailing vessels, early settlement took place on the leeward, or western side of the island, and there is a marked contrast between the small holdings on the leeward side of the island, especially between Castries and Soufrière, and the larger holdings on the windward coast. Some 130 mostly smaller holdings had been granted to poor white settlers or to free 'gens de couleurs'. The Lefort de Latour map also reveals the beginnings of the family land tenure system, as many holdings were marked as owned by 'les héritiers de' rather than by individuals. In 1787 some 56,715 hectares had been granted. Land that was not cultivated reverted to the Crown after a certain period of time and many of the holdings on the higher slopes had not been cultivated by 1787 because of their inaccessibility. A total of 773 holdings was surveyed of which 140 had reverted to the Crown and 633 were in cultivation.

When the British recaptured the island in 1803 they promised to respect the existing property ownership. Land which was marked with the name of an owner on the 1787 map, even if unoccupied, could not be disposed of until it had been escheated by the Government. This process took place very slowly and in 1922 the total amount of unalienated land, including Crown Land, amounted to 6,880 hectares or about half the island. By 1937 much of this land was in private freehold ownership leaving only about 4,000 hectares of Crown Land, which was largely the area described as a forest preserve on Lefort de Latour's map, stretching 200 paces (213 metres) on either side of the main crests and ridges of the central part of the island.

Lefort de Latour's 1787 survey provides the first detailed description of land use on St Lucia. He shows that 198 holdings were planted with cotton, whilst another 34 former sugar plantations were being planted with cotton during the period of the survey. There were 45 coffee plantations, 30 cocoa plantations and 6 with only pasture while 277 properties grew a variety of crops. Most of the tree crops were grown on the leeward coast and Lefort de Latour thought the area around Soufrière was the most suitable for the production of coffee and cocoa despite the fact that the town had been destroyed in the hurricane of 1780. Today this is the only area of the island where there is still some production of coffee and cocoa. In 1780 there had been around one hundred sugar estates but by 1787, although there were seventy-one sugar mills on the island, only forty-five estates were still growing sugar as a sole crop. Two years later this number had fallen to forty-three following the 1788 hurricane and an earthquake in which 900 people are believed to have died. However, sugar production was to increase significantly after the British took over the island, since they had less interest in coffee and cotton than the French and encouraged the monoculture of sugar cane. By 1843, according to Henry Breen, there were eighty-one sugar estates and twenty coffee plantations although not more than one-sixteenth of the island was under cultivation.

During the French Revolution the island was designated 'The Faithful' because of the support it gave to the Revolution. In 1794 the British forces recaptured the island but it was taken again in 1795, by Victor Hugues, the republican and friend of Robespierre. Captured once more by the British but restored to France at the Treaty of Amiens in 1802, the island was reclaimed by the British in 1803 and finally ceded to Great Britain in 1814. During this period the economy of the island suffered because the slaves who were freed by the French Republicans in 1794 were then returned to bondage under the British. They left the plantations and carried on guerrilla warfare as 'Brigands' until a peace was negotiated in 1797. The next few years saw a marked growth of the free coloured population from 1,878 in 1810 to 3,871 in 1825 while the numbers of both black and white inhabitants declined.

In St Lucia the number of slaves, on whose labour sugar production depended, fell from 16,000 in 1787 to 13,291 in 1834, at emancipation. At this time St Lucia had more small freehold properties than the other Windward Islands but post-emancipation expansion did not proceed very rapidly. In 1845 St Lucia had 1,345 small farms increasing slowly to 2,343 in 1853. However, there was plenty of Crown Land on which to squat and many estates also rented out land to former slaves. It is not surprising that planters complained of labour shortages. Heavily indebted, they attempted to force down the already low wages for agricultural work but in response the labourers withdrew their labour and forced the planters to return to the earlier wage levels. To overcome the shortage of labour the practice of sharecropping was introduced in 1840 and by 1844 it was reported that there were 594 acres cultivated under this system. Nevertheless, this did not prevent labour disturbances in 1849 when several estates were burned by rioters. Labour was sought from a variety of sources overseas including Germany in 1840 and Sierra Leone in 1849 and 1850. Between 1858 and 1893 4,400 workers were brought from India, of whom 2,146 were repatriated after completing their indenture.

The period from the abolition of slavery until the end of the century was one of difficulty and continuing economic crisis. Both yellow fever and smallpox were prevalent and local government was corrupt. In 1847 the nominee refused the offer of the Lieutenant-Governorship of the island and the following year the inhabitants unsuccessfully petitioned the Secretary of State because they were unable to raise the amount of money required for taxes. In 1831 the eighty-one estates on the island were heavily encumbered with mortgages for over a million pounds sterling and between 1833 and 1844 seventy-six of these estates changed hands. The general level of poverty among planters discouraged the adoption of labour-saving innovations although the first steam-driven sugar mill was set up in 1847. In 1838 the use of the French language was officially abolished and in 1840 English became the language of the Courts although French Patois remained the language of the people. Considerable emigration took place in response to opportunities elsewhere, especially in Cayenne, Panama and Cuba.

Sharecropping enabled sugar-cane acreage to increase so that by 1865 there were more acres planted than at emancipation and sugar production had increased from 2,700 tonnes in 1835 to 4,100 tonnes in 1865. St Lucia was the first of the Windward Islands to set up a Central Sugar Factory company in 1874. The centre of sugar-cane production moved south from the Castries area to Soufrière, which was also the main area for cocoa and coffee production. The acreage devoted to the cultivation of food crops declined throughout this period. Cocoa was at first largely a peasant crop but, at the beginning of the twentieth century, plantations began to grow it and for most of the next half century it occupied more land than cane. Other tree crops such as limes, coconuts and even rubber were introduced, although limes were decimated by disease in the 1920s and never really recovered. Sugar-cane production went into terminal decline after some of the best land was taken over for a military base in 1941 and the last sugar crop was produced in 1964.

Bananas began to be an important crop in St Lucia after the First World War. There had been some earlier export of bananas to Barbados but the new trade was largely carried out with Canada and the United States. In 1923 the Swift Banana Company acquired Vannard Estate in Ravine Poisson in the upper Roseau valley and plantation production of bananas began, based on the Gros Michel cultivar. Panama disease appeared on the island in 1924 and in order to avoid the ravages of the disease, bananas were planted on new land wherever possible, which solution in turn led to rapid deforestation and serious soil erosion. During the Second World War the banana-carrying boats were sunk by enemy action and banana exports ceased. In the post-war period attempts were made to revive the industry based on the relatively Panama disease-resistant Lacatan and Robusta cultivars but it was not until 1954, when Geest Industries (WI) Limited signed a contract for the regular shipment of Windward Islands bananas to Britain, that the industry really developed.

Settlement

Eighteenth-century planning laid out settlements around the coast and each of the eleven administrative quarters had a port. When communication was dependent on sailing vessels windward coastal settlements suffered; the town of Dauphin in north-west St Lucia, a centre of cotton production in the eighteenth century, had been abandoned by the nineteenth century, although there was an attempt by the ex-slaves to re-establish the settlement in the 1840s. Generally the ex-slaves in St Lucia preferred to live in the established villages or in dispersed squatter settlements in the interior. Only two new villages were founded in the decade following full emancipation, one near Vieux Fort and the other in the interior of Choiseul. There was a further expansion of rural settlement onto uncultivated land in the centre of the island after the 1914–18 War when non-agricultural employment declined and banana production offered new opportunities.

The capital town of Castries has long dominated the island's settlement pattern because of its excellent harbour. Between 1766 and 1768 the principal fort was moved from Vigie to Morne Fortuné and the town which had at first grown up to the right of the harbour was transferred to its present locality. In 1784 it was named Castries after Maréchal de Castries, the French Minister for the Navy and the Colonies. Throughout its history a number of disasters have affected Castries' development and in 1796 the first of four major fires destroyed the town. Another fire destroyed part of the town in 1813 and in October 1817 a hurricane blew down Government House burying the governor and many others in its ruins. In 1839 an earthquake damaged several buildings in Castries including the Catholic Church and the government offices. After the disastrous fire of 1948 the town was rebuilt to a new plan, streets were widened and the commercial centre and government offices reconstructed of concrete. Only the area to the south of Columbus Square was saved and here one can see a 400-year-old Saman tree and three-storey wooden buildings in the French style dating from the late nineteenth century. In 1921 the population of Castries was only 5,899, a mere 11.5 per cent of the island's population, but by 1990 39.7 per cent of the population (60,000 people), lived in the capital city.

Vieux Fort on the southern tip of the island, named after a fort supposedly built by either the Dutch or the French in the early seventeenth century, is the island's second town and its industrial centre as well as the site of the international airport. In 1921 only 2.8 per cent (1,417) of the island's total population lived in Vieux Fort but in 1990 it had 14,000 inhabitants (9.3 per cent of the population). The town of Soufrière on the west coast was founded in 1713 and used to be the second town of the island. During the French Revolution the guillotine was set up in its main square by the Brigands but the major local landowners were protected by loyal slaves and escaped. In 1921 with a population of 2,480 it had more people than Vieux Fort but by 1990 only 9,000 lived there or 6 per cent of the island's total population. Soufrière was once the major agricultural centre for the island but now its beautiful setting by the Pitons and proximity to the sulphur springs makes it more important as a tourist centre. Part of *Superman II* was filmed nearby. The changes in population in these major towns are indicative of the transition of the island from a purely agricultural economy to a more diversified one in which a majority of the people live in urban centres which are becoming more occupationally differentiated.

Politics

From 1814 St Lucia was administered as a separate colony with its own Governor and appointed Executive and Legislative Councils were instituted in 1832. Then in 1838 Britain decided to administer St Lucia as a Crown Colony and part of a Windward Island Government which included Barbados, St Vincent, Grenada and Tobago, with a Governor resident in Barbados. The first elected body, the Castries Municipal Corporation, was established in 1851 with the island's historian, Henry H. Breens as mayor. In 1885 a new Windward Islands Government was set up in which St Lucia was included with St Vincent, Grenada and Tobago with the headquarters in Grenada. Tobago was separated from the Windward Islands in 1889.

Elected representatives were added to the Legislative Council in the 1920s but full adult suffrage was not introduced until 1951, the year in which the St Lucia Labour Party (SLP) gained power, retaining it until 1964 when the United Workers' Party (UWP) won the election and governed until 1979. St Lucia gained full internal self-government in 1967 as a State in voluntary association with Britain and in 1979 became fully independent. Mr John Compton, the leader of the UWP, was Premier from 1964 to 1979 and after three years as Leader of the Opposition, won the election in 1982 and has been in power ever since. St Lucia is a bi-cameral parliamentary democracy. The House of Assembly has seventeen members while the Senate has eleven members who are appointed by the Governor General.

St Lucia is a member of the British Commonwealth, of the Caribbean Common Market (CARICOM) and of the Association of Caribbean States (ACS). It has links with Europe through its membership in the ACP Group of nations and through the Lomé agreements has received some thirty-nine million écus in assistance since 1976. St Lucia has also played a major role in regional associations. It is the administrative and research headquarters for the

Windward Island Banana Association (WINBAN) and for the Organisation of Eastern Caribbean States (OECS). Under the OECS, which comprises eight small Leeward and Windward Island Territories, the islands have established a common currency and a common central bank.

The economy

Historically, St Lucia was unusual among West Indian colonies in that it was not entirely dependent on agricultural activity. Its central location and magnificent harbour lent it a strategic importance which was exploited in a variety of ways. In the 1880s the transfer of the British military base from Barbados to St Lucia and the coaling trade provided local employment. However, the base was closed in 1906 and the coaling trade declined with the opening of the Panama Canal and the replacement of coal by oil although a small amount continued into the 1950s. The setting up of an American air base at Vieux Fort in 1941 brought new employment opportunities. In the post-war period the rebuilding of Castries, after the fire of 1948, ensured full employment for the next five years. Following this, in the mid-fifties, the banana boom provided employment and wealth and by 1957 bananas had overtaken sugar as the island's major export.

Bananas brought a new commoditization of agricultural land and the traditional system of family land tenure was seen as preventing development. Under this system land is held jointly and it was thought to make it difficult for farmers to obtain credit if they did not have freehold ownership. On the other hand, it has been argued that the family land system protected access to land for a large number of people. Recently a land titling programme has been completed.

Banana cultivation not only introduced widespread changes in the economic system but it was also the cause of significant social restructuring. Bananas elevated St Lucia from its position as one of the slums of the Commonwealth, known for its appalling record in health and education, to a situation of widespread relative prosperity. Isolated rural settlements became linked by new feeder roads and by the 1980s most people had a water supply (eighty-three per cent) and electricity (eighty-one per cent). The rigid system of social stratification typical of plantation societies was modified and an independent peasantry, proud to be banana farmers and backed by a strong producers' association, was created. The poor labour relations that had characterized the sugar industry and the coaling trade appeared to fade away as did interest in unionization. Today 96.8 per cent of banana farmers cultivate less than ten acres each but produce

69.2 per cent of the bananas exported. Thus this industry has brought small farmers into the global economy.

Bananas can be harvested throughout the year and therefore provide a steady income for small growers. St Lucia produces more bananas than any of the other Windward Islands and they constitute seventy per cent of the island's exports. Consequently the advent of the single European market in 1992 posed a major threat to the island's prosperity as they faced the loss of their protected market in Britain. St Lucia is a high-cost producer and although the island's farmers were able to secure a quota under Regulation 404/93 the market is now far more open to competition. This uncertainty, combined with the depreciation in the pound sterling to which banana prices are linked, shortages of agricultural inputs and drought in 1993, led to a farmer's strike, riots and two deaths. Banana production fell by eleven per cent and receipts by twenty-five per cent; because of the multiplier effect this was felt throughout the island. In addition, the Banana Growers Association is facing reorganization, the number of banana growers has declined to about one-quarter of the 1960s level, and the long-standing relationship with Geest as the shipper and marketing agent has changed. The future seems to lie in agricultural diversification into specialist crops with a growing appreciation of the need to link agriculture with tourism.

Tourism

Mass tourism was slow in coming to St Lucia, but once an international airport capable of taking jumbo jets was opened, many large hotels were also built. Today St Lucia has 3,000 hotel rooms available and is one of the few Caribbean territories in which European tourists are the largest group of visitors. The island has developed a distinctive type of tourism with innovative health tourism, all-inclusive resorts and ecotourism fostered by local conservationists. In the 1990s tourism has grown by eleven per cent per year and in 1993 was the biggest foreign exchange earner, bringing in EC$570 million. Seasonality is no longer a major problem and tourism is now the country's biggest single employer, although more links with other sectors of the local economy are needed.

Industry

St Lucia has the largest and most diversified manufacturing sector in the Windward Islands with about 200 companies in 1989 producing clothing, toys, sports wear, electronic goods, food and furniture. Data processing firms also exist and an oil transshipment terminal has been established. In addition, the government has built several industrial estates and is promoting industrial development. About twenty per cent of the workforce is now engaged in manufacturing. Many of the jobs available are for young women, which continues the pattern of the past when it was women porters who headloaded coal and later bananas onto ships at dockside.

Population and culture

The population of St Lucia has long been known for its poor health and education standards and its high fertility rate. Although improvements have occurred, even in the 1990s one-fifth of the population is illiterate and there is a high dependency ratio with nearly half the population under the age of fifteen. Birthrates have fallen from 30.8 per 1,000 in 1985 to 24.6 per 1,000 in 1989 and in 1991 a public education programme aimed at further reducing this rate was introduced. St Lucia was once one of the worst places in the Western hemisphere for schistosomiasis (bilharzia) and thus attracted a major long-term research project aimed at eradicating the disease. Today most of the tropical diseases which in colonial times prevented settlement expansion are no longer prevalent.

Nevertheless, this island, which in many ways has been seen as relatively backward, has produced the only Caribbean Nobel Laureates: Sir W. Arthur Lewis in economics and Derek Walcott for poetry. This paradox of intellectual superstardom arising from a small population that is generally impoverished and ill-educated is most striking. Part of the answer may lie in the tensions created by the island's colonial history. The lack of a long period under the plantation system combined with the rich dialectics of French and English traditions has enabled a strong and distinctive culture to survive. In the 1950s and 1960s this culture was fostered under the charismatic leadership of Harold Simmonds whose life was tragically cut short. He encouraged local intellectuals and artists such as Garth St Omer and raised awareness of St Lucian festivals and societies.The preservation of folk traditions and customs and of endemic flora and fauna and the study of St Lucian Creole became matters of national importance and the focus of a national identity.

Today once again St Lucia is at a crossroads. There is a protected banana market only until the year 2000 and so further diversification of the economy is urgent. However, care must be taken to ensure that this is not carried out in ways which will destroy the distinctive landscape and culture of the island.

I first saw St Lucia in 1963, at dawn, from the deck of an inter-island steamer after a night spent on a pile of ropes. Like Froude and Pope-Hennessy, I fell in love with the view as we sailed into Castries harbour, but unlike them I was not disillusioned on landing. That year I saw the 199th and final sugar cane crop in the fields and walked miles along empty beaches and rocky coasts. I saw the Pitons and tasted a St Lucia mango for the first time. Two years later I returned and met with Harold Simmonds and Garth St Omer and was taken to view and admire their portraits. Since then I have been back many times in various capacities: as a tourist; as a researcher; and as a consultant to the Windward Island Banana Growers Association. Putting together this bibliography has enabled me to relive many of these experiences.

The bibliography

I agreed to undertake this bibliography at a time when I was about to move from an academic post in Britain to one in the United States, circumstances that made the task of compilation more difficult than I at first imagined. One major problem was the lack of access to my own considerable Caribbean library which had to be stored for two years and is still being unpacked now. Nevertheless, this itinerant period did enable me to consult libraries in London, California, Barbados, Jamaica and St Lucia.

Despite its strategic importance at various periods and its cultural distinctiveness and regional leadership today there is surprisingly little written about St Lucia. In this bibliography I have attempted to identify everything published in English about the island which is available in major libraries or by inter-library loan, is a key work, is considered to be useful to the interested reader and, where technical, is also understandable and makes an important contribution for non-specialist readers. Items in which St Lucia was identified only as one of the Windward Islands were not included. Theses and reports where clearly available in microfilm form or in specialist libraries were listed by category.

I have largely excluded reports of government ministries except where they focus on censuses or similar major sources of information or provide information about the island not available elsewhere. The many publications of Sir Arthur Lewis, the poems of Derek Walcott and the novels of Garth St Omer have in general not been abstracted individually. However, the work of these brilliant and internationally known St Lucians is mentioned in several sections so that the interested reader can pursue the topic further.

Introduction

The classification scheme followed is broadly that found in other volumes of ABC-CLIO's *World Bibliographical Series*. However, certain categories have been merged or expanded reflecting their importance in the literature on St Lucia. The banana industry and tourism have been given separate categories because of their dominant position in the island's economy. Publications on land tenure also have a separate section because of the interest in the controversial topic of family land and the repeated attempts at land settlement in the island. The section on language mainly concerns the use of St Lucian Patois which after more than a century of official ostracism is now being actively fostered. Birds have a separate and substantial sub-section under flora and fauna because of the globally recognized importance of the St Lucia parrot and other endemic birds.

Other classes have been amalgamated because of a lack of published works on these topics. Among the principal categories of this nature were finance, banking and trade; education, science and technology; and directories, yearbooks and handbooks. Some categories had virtually nothing published on them. Despite, or perhaps because of the longstanding overwhelming dominance of the Roman Catholic religion and of cricket as a major sport, neither religion nor sport have been much written about. The categories of libraries, museums, books, professional periodicals and the mass media are limited by the small population, high levels of illiteracy and bilingualism.

Acknowledgements

My thanks go to all those who have aided in the preparation of this book. I would especially like to thank my research assistant, Galen Martin, who as co-author of another ABC-CLIO publication, brought his expertise to bear on this volume. He went to great lengths to exhaust the enormous facilities of the various libraries of the University of California in his search for items to be included.

Librarians were generally of great assistance. In London, especially at the Royal Commonwealth Society and the Institute of Commonwealth Studies, in Barbados in the library of the Institute of Social and Economic Studies, the library of the Caribbean Bank, of the Women and Development Unit and of Bellairs Research Institute, in Jamaica in the University Library's West India collection and the Institute of Social and Economic Studies, and in St Lucia, I was unstintingly helped. I am also grateful to my friends and co-researchers on St Lucia who responded so willingly to requests for copies of their relevant publications. Although I did not seek grants specifically for this work, my visits to the Caribbean during which some of this work was done, were funded in 1992 by the Universities of Newcastle-upon-Tyne and of California at Davis and in 1994 by the United Nations University.

Janet Momsen
Davis, California,
September 1995.

The Country and Its People

1 **The other side of paradise: foreign control in the Caribbean.**
Tom Barry, Beth Wood, Deb Preusch.   New York: The Resource Center,
Grove Press, 1984. 405p. (The Grove Press Latin America Series).
Looks at the impact on the peoples of the region of international corporate investment.
Focusing on bilateral aid, tourism, mineral exploitation and the militarization of the
Caribbean, the authors document the link between foreign investment and local
politics. St Lucia is profiled in relation to tourism, assembly industries and export
production of bananas.

2 **The Caribbean connection.**
Robert Chodos.   Toronto: James Lorimer & Company, 1977. 269p. map.
bibliog.
The focus in this work is on Canadian links with the Caribbean. St Lucia is viewed in
terms of its attraction to Canadians as a holiday resort and location for retirement and
the related investment in tourism through the Canadian-owned Holiday Inns and
second home development.

3 **Fifth report from the Foreign Affairs Committee: Caribbean and
Central America.**
Foreign Affairs Committee of the House of Commons.   London:
HMSO, 1982. 107p., 408p. map.
This report considers Britain's changing relationship with the Caribbean in the light of
increased United States involvement in the region and Britain's membership of the
European Community. The effect of this change on newly independent St Lucia is
considered and preferential access to the European market for bananas is seen as an
impending problem. St Lucia needs continuing financial support and in 1980 received
£923,000 of aid from Britain. The Oxfam representative stated that St Lucia was one
of its priority areas for funding in the region, along with the other Windwards islands
and Haiti.

1

4   **St Lucia: a supplement to the West Indies Chronicle.**
London: West India Committee, 1975. 56p. map.

Provides an illustrated description of the island and its people in the early 1970s with
an introduction by Premier John G. M. Compton. Despite the collapse of the British-
owned Court Line, the owner of the largest hotel in St Lucia, new hotels have opened
and the island's tourist industry is flourishing. The increase in world oil prices
stimulated the government of St Lucia to drill for thermal energy in the area of the
Sulphur Springs near Soufrière.

5   **St Lucia: a supplement to the West Indies Chronicle.**
Edited by David Jessop.   London: West India Committee, 1978. 41p.

Illustrated with many monochrome and colour photographs, this supplement consists
of a series of articles describing the current situation in agriculture, manufacturing and
tourism. David Jessop also interviews Premier Compton about independence, the
economy and the political scene. Overall it is considered that St Lucia is the best
equipped economically of all the Associated States to cope with the strains created by
independence.

6   **Storm signals: structural adjustment and development alternatives in
the Caribbean.**
Kathy McAfee.   London: Zed Books; Boston, Massachusetts: Oxfam
America, 1991. 259p. map.

McAfee discusses development problems and alternative solutions for the Caribbean
region, with a unique focus on the impact of economic and environmental crises on
the lives of ordinary people. She provides a useful outline of the work of three St
Lucian non-governmental organizations: the Folk Research Centre founded in 1982
which has encouraged the use of Creole; CANARI which has been disseminating
participatory approaches to conservation and environmental management; and the
Staff Co-operative which helped farmers set up buyers and producers co-operatives, a
feed mill and a slaughterhouse, and make the island virtually self-sufficient in poultry
and pork products by the end of the 1980s.

7   **Britain and the United States in the Caribbean.**
Mary Proudfoot.   London: Faber & Faber, 1954. Reprinted, Westport,
Connecticut: Greenwood Press, 1976. 434p. map. bibliog.

Written by an Oxford historian married to an American, this was one of the first books
published about the post-war situation in the Caribbean. It is based on fieldwork
carried out in Barbados, Jamaica, Trinidad, St Lucia, Puerto Rico and the United
States Virgin Islands from 1949 to 1950 and focuses on a comparison of the methods
of administration of colonies and dependencies employed by Britain and the United
States. A number of detailed appendices are included based largely on the 1946 census
returns. This is a valuable study for those interested in Caribbean social conditions of
the period.

8   **Time for action: the report of the West Indian Commission.**
Sir Sridath Ramphal, Commission Chairman.   Black Rock, Barbados:
The West Indian Commission, 1992. 592p.

The Commission was set up in 1989 to consider the situation of the Caribbean in the
21st century in the light of the ending of the Cold War. Information was gathered
through consultation with individuals and communities throughout the Caribbean and
the diaspora. The report is organized in three parts: the first reviews the CARICOM
experience and considers its future role; the second contains eight chapters on specific
problems of the contemporary Caribbean; and the third part sets out a programme for
strengthening the Caribbean community by both deepening and widening the process
of integration. The role of St Lucia in the integrative efforts of the Organization of
Eastern Caribbean States is seen as a positive aspect.

9   **West Indies.**
Philip Sherlock.   London: Thames & Hudson, 1966. 215p. maps.
bibliog. (New Nations and Peoples Library).

Written while the author was Vice-Chancellor of the University of the West Indies,
this study focuses on the islands which had been or still were British colonies shortly
after the Federation of the West Indies collapsed. It includes a regional fact sheet and
a 'Who's Who'. St Lucia is specifically considered in terms of its use of creole, its
history of strikes and its dependence on bananas.

10 **St Lucia.**
Richard Tolson, David L. Niddrie, Janet D. Momsen.   In : *The New
Encyclopaedia Britannica*, vol. 29.   Chicago: Encyclopaedia
Britannica Inc., 1990, p. 772-74.

Covers the topography, climate, population, economy, administration, social
conditions, politics and history of St Lucia.

11 **The West Indies: patterns of development, culture and
environmental change since 1492.**
David Watts.   Cambridge, England: Cambridge University Press, 1987.
609p. maps. bibliog.

In this pan-Caribbean environmental history of the region Watts focuses on the
plantation period of 1492-1900. St Lucia is mentioned mainly in relation to the
numerous changes in French and British political control and the decline of sugar
production. Some 200 plantations were abandoned between 1799 and 1817 because of
shortages of slave labour.

The Caribbean in transition.
See item no. 126.

A post-emancipation history of the West Indies.
See item no. 127.

The memoirs of Père Labat, 1693-1705.
See item no. 128.

The Caribbean: the genesis of a fragmented nationalism.
See item no. 129.

West Indian societies.
See item no. 174.

Economic and political change in the Leeward and Windward Islands.
See item no. 261.

Geography

General

12 **The Caribbean Islands: endless geographical diversity.**
Thomas Boswell, Dennis Conway. New Brunswick, New Jersey:
Rutgers University Press, 1992. 218p. maps.
Includes a chapter on St Lucia, which constitutes day eight of a ten-day, socially
conscious tour itinerary for the Caribbean. The St Lucia chapter includes geographical
information, a brief history of the island, comments on the forest industry, and a
discussion of eco-tourism.

13 **The Lesser Antilles.**
William Morris Davies. New York: American Geographical Society,
1926. 207p. maps. bibliog. (American Geographical Society Map of
Hispanic America, publication no. 2).
The author of this work who was the leading American geomorphologist of his time,
provides a basic introduction to the structural history and contemporary physical form
of the islands of the Lesser Antillean arc. St Lucia fits into this category, based on
volcanic processes, which also accounts for most of the other islands. Sixty-six line
diagrams and sixteen black-and-white plates are included.

14 **West Indies.**
David Lowenthal. In: *McGraw-Hill encyclopedia of science and
technology*. New York: McGraw-Hill, 1960, p. 473-76.
Discusses the physical environment, population and political status of the Bahamas
and the Greater and Lesser Antilles. The Pitons in St Lucia are noted as the most
spectacular volcanic peaks.

15   **The geography of land use and population in the Caribbean (with special reference to Barbados and the Windward Islands).**
Janet D. Momsen.   PhD thesis, University of London, 1970. 564p.
maps. bibliog. (Available from Senate House, University of London).

The first part describes the historical development of land occupancy and land use in Barbados, Martinique, Grenada, St Vincent, Dominica and St Lucia. In the second half a quantitative factorial analysis of small-scale agriculture based on questionnaire surveys in all six islands is presented. The influence of French and British colonial policies on island agriculture is compared.

16   **The Caribbean in the wider world, 1492-1992: a regional geography.**
Bonham C. Richardson.   Cambridge, England: Cambridge University Press, 1992. 235p. maps. bibliog.

Richardson takes a world systems approach to the place of the Caribbean in the world economy. St Lucia is mentioned in relation to its dependency on the export of bananas and the migration of its people to assist in building the Panama Canal.

17   **Commercial geography of St Lucia.**
Otis P. Starkey.   Bloomington, Indiana: Indiana University, Department of Geography, for the Office of Naval Research, 1961. 15p. maps. bibliog. (Technical Report, no. 8).

Provides a description of St Lucia in 1960 covering the island's physical setting, economic history, population (based on the 1946 census), agricultural structure and production (based on the 1956-58 agricultural survey), forestry, fishing, manufacturing, public utilities, trade, transport and outlook for the future.

The West Indies: patterns of development, culture and environmental change since 1492.
See item no. 11.

West Indian societies.
See item no. 174.

Maps and atlases

18   **1778 plan of St Lucia in the West Indies.**
Thomas Bowen.   London: [n.p.], 1778.

The map shows attacks made on 13-16 December 1778, and includes a descriptive text. The actual size of the map is nineteen by twenty-six centimetres, drawn at a scale of approximately 1:51,000. Relief is shown by hachures and the map is oriented with north to the left.

19   **St Lucia holiday and general guide map 74/75.**
Castries: Publishers & Promoters, 1974.

This tourist-oriented map measures thirty-six by eighteen centimetres with a scale of
1:120,000. The planimetric map shows roads, rivers, boundaries and main towns on
the island, whilst the margins contain text, tables and illustrations. On the reverse of
the map is a Castries city plan and directory.

20   **St Lucia.**
Directorate of Overseas Surveys.   Tolworth, England: Directorate of
Overseas Surveys, 1958.

Based on aerial photographs taken in 1951 and 1955, this is a topographical map in
three sheets at a scale of 1:25,000.

21   **Saint Lucia, the West Indies (revised edition).**
Directorate of Overseas Surveys.   Tolworth, England: Directorate of
Overseas Surveys, 1965. (DOS 445, Series E703).

This is a colour map, measuring ninety-five by sixty-four centimetres and using the
Transverse Mercator projection. Relief is shown by hill shading, contours, and spot
heights. The scale is 1:50,000 with an inset of Castries at a scale of 1:10,000. The
margins contain a sheet history, legend, grids and references.

22   **St Lucia tourist map.**
Directorate of Overseas Surveys.   Tolworth, England: Directorate of
Overseas Surveys, 1982.

At a scale of 1:50,000 and based on a 1980 survey, this tourist map also has an inset
map of Castries at 1:12,500, an index of buildings and an inset of the whole
Caribbean. The margins contain tourist information.

23   **Road map of St Lucia.**
John Erlinger-Ford.   Castries, 1961.

Erlinger-Ford's map shows both paved and unpaved roads and has a scale of one inch
to one and half miles.

24   **Carte géometrique et géographique de l'Isle Ste Lucie, 1787.**
(Geometrical and geographical map of the island of St Lucia, 1787).
M. Lefort de Latour.   London: Colonial Office, 1787. Reprinted, 1883.
(Colonial Office Maps, St Lucia, no. 9).

Drawn up to accompany his brief written account, *A general description of the island
of St Lucia, 1787* (see item no. 298), this map shows land ownership, land tenure and
land use in 1787. The scale is at one inch to 0.33 miles.

25 **St Lucia: banana lands.**
Janet D. Momsen.   London: Directorate of Overseas Surveys, 1969.
At a scale of 1:50,000, this map, which accompanies item no. 360, depicts banana
lands with green shading. Banana areas are classified according to density of growth
and crop mix.

26 **St Lucia.**
United States Central Intelligence Agency.   Washington, DC: The
Agency, 1991.
This is a colour map measuring twenty-one centimetres by seventeen. Relief is shown
by shading and spot heights and the scale is 1:300,000. An inset location map is
included.

St Lucia historic sites.
See item no. 137.

A history of the voyages and travels of Captain N. Uring.
See item no. 148.

Bibliographic survey of Latin America and the Caribbean, 1969.
See item no. 527.

Geology and Soils

Geology and geomorphology

27   Preliminary geochemical and thermodynamic assessment of the geothermal resources, Sulphur Springs area, St Lucia, W. I.
F. D'Amore, J. R. Rivera, D. Giusti, R. Rossi. *Applied Geochemistry*, vol. 5 (1990), p. 587-604.

Reports on a high-temperature geothermal resource which was tapped by means of a well 1,410 metres deep. The well encountered mainly dactic agglomerates and lava flows and a permeable zone below 1,340 metres, with a maximum temperature of approximately 290°C. A decline in reservoir pressure of about fifteen per cent was observed at the end of the production test. Technical information on well output is provided.

28   Geothermal energy in St Lucia.
Anon. *Raw Materials Report,* vol. 6, no. 4 (1989), p. 16-19.

Describes the role of the United Nations Revolving Fund for Natural Resources Exploration in developing geothermal energy in St Lucia in order to meet the needs of rural electrification. Since 1982 almost US$10 million has been spent on the project and two wells have been drilled.

29   Evidence for fluid bodies beneath the Sulphur Springs geothermal region, St Lucia, West Indies.
W. P. Aspinall, M. O. Michael, J. F. Tomblin. *Geophysical Research Letters*, vol. 3, no. 2 (1976), p. 87-90.

Discusses the extent of the hot springs' resources in St Lucia.

30   **The Sulphur Springs geothermal field, St Lucia, Lesser Antilles: hydrothermal mineralogy of wells SL-1 and SL-2.**
      S. Battaglia, G. Gianelli, R. Rossi, G. Cavarretta.   *Journal of South American Earth Sciences*, vol. 4, no. 1/2 (1991), p. 1-12.

The authors describe how two wells drilled in St Lucia's geothermal field reveal a complex volcanic sequence, which is characterized by collapse episodes followed by the emplacement of dacite domes. The alteration of mineral assemblages indicates that the hydrothermal system has cooled at the levels sampled. Current well-bottom temperatures are around 270-90°C

31   **Determining the significance of landslide activity: examples from the Eastern Caribbean.**
      Jerome V. de Graff.   *Caribbean Geography*. vol. 3, no. 1 (1991),
      p. 29-42.

Drawing on field data from St Vincent, Dominica and St Lucia, the author describes the effects of landslides on the peoples and economies of the Eastern Caribbean. He demonstrates how landslide impacts can be determined and presents mitigation measures for landslide risk reduction.

32   **Caribbean island springs a hot surprise.**
      New Scientist, vol. 117, no. 1,603 (10 March 1988), p. 37.

Reports on a project, backed by the United Nations natural resources fund, to bring geothermal power to St Lucia. An international team of engineers drilled a 1,500-metre well in the Sulphur Springs area, which produced a mixture of steam and superheated water at 300°C. Initial results indicated that a single bore could provide for up to half the island's energy needs but it was later decided that the resource was not large enough to be economic.

33   **Some heat measurements in West Indian Soufrières.**
      G. R. Robson, P. L. Willmore.   *Bulletin Volcanologique*, series 2,
      vol. 17 (1975), p. 13-39.

Includes measurements taken in the Qualibou Soufrière of St Lucia.

34   **Volcanic history and petrology of the Soufrière region, St Lucia.**
      John F. Tomblin.   DPhil thesis, University of Oxford, England, 1964.
      maps. bibliog.

This was the first detailed study of the history of vulcanism in St Lucia focusing on the youngest volcanics in the south-west of the island. Tomblin identifies the caldera as being at least 50,000 years old, while the youngest major pumice flow was dated at 39,050 years BP. Chemical analyses of twenty volcanic rocks from St Lucia are included.

35 **Economic geological resources of the Leeward and Windward Islands.**
J. F. Tomblin, J. E. Tomblin. Tolworth, England: British Geological Survey Overseas Division, 1987. 177p. bibliog.
Discusses the use of geothermal heat in St Lucia for the agro-industry and for brick- and tile-making.

36 **Large role of sediments in the genesis of some Lesser Antilles andesites and dacites (Soufrière, St Lucia): isotropic constraints.**
Philippe Vidal, Martine Le Guen de Kerneizon, René C. Maury, Bernard Dupré, William M. White. *Bulletin de la Société Géologique de France*, vol. 162, no. 6 (1991), p. 993-1,002.
This study of the source of orogenic andesitic magma discusses samples of andesites and dacites from the Soufrière volcano in St Lucia which reveal that, in contrast to the majority of the Lesser Antillean volcanics, a sedimentary component has played a very significant role in their generation. The strontium-oxygen isotopic relationship suggests a mixing model between sediments and oceanic crust in the subduction zone, that is, source contamination, rather than crustal contamination during magma ascent.

Soils

37 **Geostatistical analysis of soil properties in a secondary tropical dry forest, St Lucia, West Indies.**
Otto J. Gonzalez, Donald R. Zak. *Plant and Soil*, vol. 163 (1994), p. 45-54.
Spatial variability of soil properties directly influences forest growth. In this study of a relatively undisturbed area of tropical dry forest on the east coast of St Lucia, samples were collected at four-mile intervals and used as the basis for maps of soil properties. Most soil properties exhibited spatial autocorrelation at distances of twenty-four miles or less. Fine-scale patterns of net nitrification are likely to have been driven by overstory litter inputs rather than variation in soil texture, mineralogy and water availability. No similarity was found between soil texture or pH and other properties.

38 **Runoff and soil loss from strip cropped and terraced hillside lands in St Lucia.**
C. A. Madramootoo, P. Norville. *Journal of Agricultural Engineering Research*, vol. 55 (1993), p. 239-49.
Soil erosion is especially severe on most Caribbean islands because of steep terrain, erosion-prone soils, deforestation and high rainfall intensities. Indeed, in St Lucia severe erosion leading to landslides and avalanches on hillside banana plantations has occurred. The authors discuss two soil conservation systems which were designed and installed for small-scale banana production on hillslopes. Rainfall, run-off and soil

loss were measured during twenty-four storms in the 1988 wet season and it was found that generally there was more run-off and soil loss from the strip cropped plot than from the terraced plot.

39 **The design and evaluation of soil conservation systems in St Lucia.**
Peter Norville. MSc thesis, McGill University, Montreal, Quebec, 1989. bibliog. (Available from University Microfilms International, Ann Arbor, Michigan, order no. DA MM63732).

Norville presents a study of three soil conservation systems (contour drainage, strip cropping and terracing) which were designed and established within separate plots on hillside farmlands in St Lucia. A control plot with no form of conservation was also set up. Rainfall, run-off and soil loss were measured over one wet season and crop yields and construction and maintenance costs were determined. Norville reports that the largest amounts of run-off were from the strip cropped plot and soil loss was least in the control plot. Construction costs were highest for the terraced plot.

40 **Soil and land use surveys no. 20, St Lucia.**
J. Stark, P. Lajoie, A. J. Green. Trinidad: University of the West Indies, Imperial College of Tropical Agriculture, Soil Research and Survey Section of the Regional Research Centre, 1966. 50p. maps.

The first part of this survey describes the various factors affecting the land use of St Lucia: climate; geology and lithology; relief and drainage; vegetation; agriculture; and services. The second part focuses on soils and their capabilities and the third part suggests an optimum soil capability programme and future research directions. There are three appendices detailing soil characteristics, acreages, slope and profiles.

41 **Notes on a botanical and soil inspection of the St Lucia banana and forest lands.**
C. W. Wardlaw. *Tropical Agriculture*, vol. 6, no. 2 (1929), p. 304-09.

The author observes that banana field abandonment is a function of both disease and progressive soil deterioration due to a variety of causes set in motion by deforestation and continuous cropping. He also describes the system of 'peasant gardens' which he finds to be exceedingly destructive and compares the soils of cultivated areas to the soils and regeneration processes of virgin forest land. Wardlaw concludes that the regeneration of deteriorated land by natural processes is slow and doubtful.

42 **A synthesis of soil classifications used in the Central Lesser Antilles.**
Barbara Welch. *Soil Survey and Land Evaluation*, vol. 7 (1987), p. 1-11. maps. bibliog.

Develops a composite soil classification for St Lucia, Dominica, Martinique and Guadeloupe which allows a comparison of soil resources between the French and Commonwealth Islands despite the fact that their soil surveys use different classifications. The composite classification system is based on the nature and degree of development of clay minerals. It was most difficult to fit St Lucia into this classification.

Flora and Fauna

Birds

43 **List of birds of the island of St Lucia, West Indies.**
J. A. Allen. *Bulletin of the Nuttall Ornithological Club,* vol. 5 (1880),
p. 163-69.
Describes three collections donated to the Museum of Comparative Zoology which
contained a total of 350 specimens. The new items from these collections, including
Loxigilla noctis sclateri, brought the total bird species known to exist on St Lucia to
fifty-six.

44 **Supplementary list of birds of the island of Santa Lucia, W. I.**
J. A. Allen. *Bulletin of the Nuttall Ornithological Club,* vol. 6 (April
1881), p. 28.
In this account of another collection of birds from St Lucia, twelve species are added,
bringing the total for the island to sixty-eight.

45 **Report of the 1987 UEA/ICBP St Lucia Expedition.**
Stephen Babbs, Sebastian Buckton, Peter Robertson, Pete Wood.
Cambridge, England: International Council for Bird Preservation, 1988.
48p. maps. bibliog. (Study Report, no. 33).
Reports on the findings of the Expedition, which was invited to St Lucia to study six
of the island's bird species. Particular emphasis was placed on the four least-known
species: the White-breasted Thrasher; the St Lucia Wren; the St Lucia Nightjar; and
the Semper's Warbler. White-breasted Thrashers are restricted to narrow bands of
riverine vegetation which are rapidly being destroyed, the St Lucia Wren was thought
to be extinct but twenty-four pairs were counted, and seven individual Nightjars were
located. No Semper's Warblers were seen, however.

46 **Behavioral and ecological comparisons of Lesser Antillean bullfinches: a study of the evolution of sexual dimorphism and monomorphism.**
Joan Ruth Bird. PhD, University of Montana, Missoula, Montana, 1983. 213p. bibliog. (Available from University Microfilms International, Ann Arbor, Michigan, order no. DA 8322851).

Compares behavioural and ecological correlates of bullfinches in Barbados, St Vincent and St Lucia. The Barbadian sub-species differed from those in St Vincent and St Lucia in foraging behaviour and it is suggested that this led to the development of significantly longer tarsi and a brown rather than black colouration of adult males in Barbados. These differences are attributed to the drier conditions found in Barbados.

47 **A new Golden Warbler from the Island of St Lucia, B. W. I.**
James Bond. *Auk,* vol. 44 (Oct. 1927), p. 571-72.

Describes the Golden Warbler *Dendroica petechia babad,* found on St Lucia.

48 **On the birds of Dominica, St Lucia, St Vincent and Barbados, B. W. I.**
James Bond. *Proceedings of the Academy of Natural Sciences of Philadelphia,* vol. 80 (1928), p. 523-45.

Bond reports on the ornithological research he carried out in St Lucia in 1927 and provides the first records for *Falco pergrinus anatum* and *Dendroica tigrina.*

49 **The rediscovery of the St Lucian Black Finch (*Melanospiza richardsoni*).**
James Bond. *Auk,* vol. 46 (Oct. 1929), p. 523-26.

Notes the rediscovery of the St Lucian Black Finch and describes the female of the species and the finch's habitat and song.

50 **Notes on some birds from St Lucia, B. W. I.**
James Bond. *Auk,* vol. 49 (Oct. 1932). p. 494-96.

Bond notes some of the rarer birds he collected in 1929, including *Troglodytes mesoleucus,* and discusses the addition of *Nephoecetes niger niger* to the list of St Lucia birds. He also provides a description of *Gallinula c. cerceris* and of the skin of *Antrostomus* received by the Philadelphia Academy from Stanley John.

51   **The St Lucia Amazon (*Amazona versicolor*): its changing status and conservation.**
P. J. Butler.   In: *Conservation of new world parrots: proceedings of the ICBP Parrot Working Group Meeting St Lucia 1980.*   Edited by Roger F. Pasquier.   Washington, DC: Smithsonian Institution Press for the International Council for Bird Preservation, 1981. Reprinted, 1982, p. 171-80. bibliog. (International Council for Bird Preservation Technical Publication, no. 1).

The St Lucia Parrot is the rarest of the four remaining Lesser Antillean amazons. It was plentiful in 1850 but by 1900 was in danger of extinction. The 1885 Wild Bird Protection Ordinance led to a small increase but by 1950 there were only 1,000 parrots left and by 1977 only about 100. The parrot is still under threat because of the destruction of its habitat and from predators such as snakes, hawks and the mongoose. A nature reserve including all the known parrot nesting sites has now been established.

52   **The crab hawk (Urubitinga) in the island of St Lucia, West Indies.**
Austin H. Clark.   *Auk*, vol. 22 (1905), p. 210.

Records a sighting of this bird at Soufrière.

53   **A list of birds of the island of St Lucia.**
Austin H. Clark.   *West India Bulletin*, vol. 11, no. 3 (1911), p. 182-93.

The author provides a list of sixty-one recorded species followed by another of forty-four species which have not yet been recorded but which might be expected to be found on the island. This is followed by a note on the protection of the indigenous birds of St Lucia and on the introduction of exotic birds.

54   **The Dwarf cowbird (*Molothrus bonariensis minimus*) in St Lucia.**
Stuart T. Danforth.   *Auk*, vol. 44 (Jan. 1932), p. 96-97.

This is the first recorded sighting of the Dwarf cowbird in St Lucia, where it was seen in Aux Coin Swamp.

55   **The birds of St Lucia.**
Stuart T. Danforth.   Rio Pedras, Puerto Rico: University of Puerto Rico, 1935. 129p. (Monographs of the University of Puerto Rico, series B, no. 6).

Based on a month's observations in St Lucia in 1931, this is the first account of the birds of any of the Lesser Antilles. St Lucia was chosen because the number of endemic birds was thought to be larger than in the other islands and many of these were considered to be verging on extinction. Seventy-eight species of birds, of which sixteen are endemic, are listed as resident in St Lucia. Two others are included on somewhat doubtful grounds and all eighty are described in detail.

56   **Habitats and feeding stations of St Lucia forest birds.**
A. W. Diamond.   *Ibis*, vol. 115 (1973), p. 313-29.

Describes the habitat and feeding patterns of such St Lucian birds as the St Lucian parrot, the forest thrush and the orioles.

57 **Birds of the Eastern Caribbean.**
Peter G. H. Evans. London; Basingstoke, England: The Macmillan
Press, 1990. 162p. map. bibliog. (Macmillan Caribbean Pocket Natural
History Series).

This is a beautifully produced book covering the birds of the region, stretching from
the Virgin Islands to Grenada. The introduction includes a brief mention of the local
ecology, conservation and bird breeding biology, and hints on Caribbean bird
watching and photography. A checklist and list of bird-watching sites for St Lucia, as
well as for twelve other areas, is included at the end. Descriptions of 180 species of
birds that either breed in or regularly visit the region are given and colour photographs
are provided of the St Lucia Nightjar and the St Lucia Parrot.

58 **Current status of and threats to some parrots of the Lesser Antilles.**
M. Gochfeld. *Biological Conservation*, vol. 3 (1974), p. 184-88.

Provides a brief survey of the status of the St Lucia Parrot (*A. versicolor*) on St Lucia
and concludes that the bird is rare and endangered.

59 **A report on the field study of the St Lucia Parrot *Amazona
versicolor* during 1975.**
D. F. Jeggo. *Jersey Wildlife Preservation Trust, Twelfth Annual
Report* (1975), p. 34-41.

Reports on a visit to St Lucia during which the first observations of the nests of the
St Lucia parrot (*A. versicolor*) were made and one nestling was taken for the captive
breeding programme.

60 **Lesser Antillean Parrot Programme, a progress report.**
D. F. Jeggo. *Jersey Wildlife Preservation Trust, Thirteenth Annual
Report* (1976), p. 21-26.

During 1976 an intensive effort was made to locate the nests of the St Lucia parrot (*A.
versicolor*). Eight active nests were found but eventually only three nests, each
containing two chicks, remained active. All six chicks were taken at the age of six
weeks for the captive breeding programme. Amazon parrots take several years to
mature and usually have only one or two chicks a year so it will be quite a long time
before the captive breeding programme can make a major contribution to the total
population of the St Lucia Parrot.

61 **The captive breeding programme for Caribbean Amazons at the
Jersey Wildlife Preservation Trust.**
D. F. Jeggo. In: *Conservation of New World parrots: proceedings of
the ICBP Parrot Working Group Meeting St Lucia 1980.* Edited by
Roger F. Pasquier. Washington, DC: Smithsonian Institution Press for
the International Council for Bird Preservation, 1981. Reprinted, 1982.
p. 181-96. bibliog. (International Council for Bird Preservation,
Technical Publication no. 1).

Reports on the captive breeding programme for the St Lucia parrot which was
established at the Jersey Wildlife Preservation Trust. The first birds were captured in

1975 and by 1978 there were nine in the programme, although no mating had occurred by 1980.

62 Captive breeding programs for *Amazona* parrots.
H. A. J. Nichols. In: *Endangered birds: management techniques for preserving threatened species.* Edited by Stanley A. Temple.
Madison, Wisconsin: University of Wisconsin Press, 1977, p. 263-71.

Reports on studies of parrots being carried out in Dominica, St Vincent and St Lucia and on the captive breeding programme being set up in Jersey.

63 Conservation strategy for parrots of the Caribbean islands.
Roger F. Pasquier. In: *Conservation of new world parrots: proceedings of the ICBP Parrot Working Group Meeting St Lucia 1980.* Edited by Roger F. Pasquier. Washington, DC: Smithsonian Institution Press for the International Council for Bird Preservation, 1981. Reprinted, 1982. p. 1-6. (International Council for Bird Preservation, Technical Publication no. 1).

Outlines the recommendations of the Parrot Working Group for parrot conservation on each island in the Caribbean. For St Lucia the first priority was the establishment of a Nature Reserve. Secondary priorities were to implement the 1975 Wildlife Ordinance and to determine the long-term effects of Hurricane Allen (1980) on population and habitat. Other recommendations were the establishment of a register of captive parrots, the institution of a breeding programme and the expansion of rainforest tourism.

64 Patterns of Shiny Cowbird parasitism in St Lucia and southwestern Puerto Rico.
William Post, Tammie K. Nakamura, Alexander Cruz. *The Condor*, vol. 92 (1990), p. 461-69.

The Shiny Cowbird (*Molothrus bonariensis*) is a generalist brood parasite, which has spread rapidly through the Caribbean reaching North America by 1985. It has lowered the reproductive output of several host species. The cowbird has been in St Lucia since at least 1931 but its distribution there is less dense than in Puerto Rico. In St Lucia four out of eight potential host species were parasitized and Cowbird parasitism reduced Yellow Warbler nest success in the island.

65 Description of a new warbler from the island of St Lucia, West Indies.
Robert Ridgeway. *Proceedings of the United States Nature Museum*, vol. 5 (1882), p. 525-26.

Provides the first description of *Dendroica adelaidae delicata*.

66   **Birds collected on the island of St Lucia, West Indies, the Abrolhos Island, Brazil and at the Straits of Magellan in 1887-88.**
Robert Ridgeway. *Proceedings of the United States Nature Museum,* vol. 12 (1890), p. 129-30.

An account of the collections made by the 'Albatross' expedition in St Lucia on 1-2 December 1887. Ridgeway lists thirty specimens representing fifteen species including *Melanospiza* and *Leucopeza*.

67   **On the birds of the island of St Lucia, West Indies.**
Philip Lutley Sclater. *Proceedings of the Zoological Society of London* (21 March 1871), p. 263-73.

Presents an account of a collection of birds received from the Reverend J. E. Semper, in which twenty-five different species were represented. This is the first published list of the birds of St Lucia. In it *Icterus laudabilis* is described as new and a coloured plate of the bird is included.

68   **On some additional species of birds from St Lucia, West Indies.**
Philip Lutley Sclater. *Proceedings of the Zoological Society of London* (1876), p. 13-14.

Reports on a third collection of birds sent by the Reverend Semper, containing eight species which had not previously been reported. *Troglodytes mesoleucus* and *Leucopeza semperi* are described as new and the latter is depicted in a colour plate.

69   **List of birds collected by Mr Ramage in St Lucia, West Indies.**
Philip Lutley Sclater. *Proceedings of the Zoological Society of London* (5 Nov. 1889), p. 394-95.

The ninety-six specimens in this account were collected by George A. Ramage and represented thirty different species. None of them were new to the list for St Lucia.

70   **Observations on the birds of St Lucia: with notes by P. L. Sclater.**
Reverend J. E. Semper. *Proceedings of the Zoological Society of London* (20 April 1872), p. 647-53.

Provides notes on the behaviour and habitat of many St Lucian birds.

71   **Save the St Lucia parrot.**
World Wildlife Fund. *The Caribbean and West Indies Chronicle,* vol. 98, no. 1,566 (Feb./March 1982), p. 21-24.

The St Lucia parrot, *Amazona versicolor,* one of the world's rarest birds, has become the key figure in a wide-ranging conservation programme. By the mid-1970s only about a hundred parrots remained because of hunting and habitat destruction. Since then a programme of nature reserves supported by effective legislation and community education has been very successful. On 23 September, 1979 the government declared the St Lucia Parrot its National Bird and followed this with a Wildlife Protection Ordinance.

Other fauna

72 **The reptiles of the Maria Islands, St Lucia: report to the Eastern Caribbean Natural Area Management Program (ECNAMP) and the World Wildlife Fund.**
David Corke. Vieux Fort, St Lucia: Eastern Caribbean Natural Area Management Program, 1983. 51p.

Based on a month's survey of the reptiles of the Maria Islands, this report places special emphasis on the endemic ground lizard. These small islands, which have been established as a nature reserve, are home to seven species of reptile, two of which are endemic to the Maria Islands. This research was undertaken to provide background information for managing the reserve.

73 **Reptile conservation on the Maria Islands (St Lucia, West Indies).**
David Corke. *Biological Conservation*, vol. 40 (1987), p. 263-79.

The twelve hectares of the two Maria Islands have a reptile fauna with a high proportion of endemic species. The islets support seven reptile species, of which four are exclusive St Lucian endemics; two of these (the lizard *Cnemidophorus vanzoi* and the colubrid snake *Liophis ornatus*) survive only on the Marias. These islets were declared a wildlife reserve by the St Lucia Government and vested in the St Lucia National Trust in 1982. The tree lizard *Anolis luciae* is present in the Maria Islands where it enjoys the absence of the introduced competitors it has to face on the mainland of St Lucia. In addition, the gecko *Hemidactylus palaichthus* was previously known only on one Maria Island but has now been reported from other islets and from mainland St Lucia. The present status of Maria Island reptiles is reviewed in this article and their conservation management discussed.

74 **The status and conservation needs of the terrestrial herpetofauna of the Windward Islands (West Indies).**
David Corke. *Biological Conservation*, vol. 62 (1992), p. 47-58.

Reports on the current status of the amphibians and reptiles of the Windward Islands. Four of the eight West Indian reptile species which have become extinct since 1660 came from the Windward Islands, although there is no evidence for the widely reported role of introduced mongooses in the decline of Windward Island's reptiles.

75 *Acugutturus parasiticus*, **new genus new species, a remarkable ectoparasitic aphelenchoid nematode from** *Periplaneta americana* **with proposal of Acugutturinae, new subfamily.**
D. J. Hunt. *Systematic Parasitology*, vol. 1, nos. 3/4 (1980), p. 167-70.

A. parasiticus, a unique species because of the length of its conus, is found in St Lucia and described here. A new subfamily *Acugutturinae* is proposed to accommodate the new genus.

76 **The isolation and characterization of three thermophilic anaerobes from a hot spring in St Lucia.**
Timothy Mark Karnauchow. MSc thesis, Queen's University, Kingston, Ontario, 1990. bibliog. (Available from University Microfilms International, Ann Arbor, Michigan, order no. DA M61491).

Considers the findings when three thermophilic anaerobes originating from a mud sample taken from a hot spring in St Lucia were isolated and characterized. The first, the St Lucia Methanogen, was an autotroph and demonstrated a number of distinguishing characteristics. Two thermophilic eubacterial bacilli were also purified. One was a saccharolytic fermentative organism and the other a peritrichously flagellated, spore-forming autotrophic sulphate reducer.

77 **Isolation and characterization of three thermophilic anaerobes from a St Lucia hot spring.**
T. M. Karnauchow, S. F. Koval, K. F. Jarrell. *Systematic Applied Microbiology*, vol. 15 (1992), p. 296-310. bibliog.

Three thermophilic anaerobes were isolated from a sample of mud from the Sulphur Springs south of Terre Blanche in St Lucia. One, a rod-shaped methanogen had a sufficient number of unique features to be designated a new strain of *Methanobacterium thermoautrophicum*. The other two were eubacterial isolates which were identified as new thermophilic members of the genera *Clostridium* and *Desulfotomaculum*.

78 **Biotics of *Biomphalaria Glabrata* (say) and associated fauna in St Lucia, West Indies.**
William Brian McKillop. PhD thesis, University of Waterloo, Canada, 1975. bibliog.

Several aspects of the ecology of the aquatic snail and its associated molluscan fauna were investigated over a two-and-a-half-year period in St Lucia and the results documented in this study. The distribution and population density of the snail was found to be related to protection from heavy rainfall and the level of nitrate concentration in the water. Most suitable sites were found to be mountainside marshes used by farmers for the cultivation of dasheen. Behavioural studies indicated that the snail, *B. glabrata*, became much more active at night and that both upstream and downstream migration occurred in the dasheen marshes. In the dry season snail populations build up in the quieter backwaters of streams and rivers through downstream drift. It is here that they come into contact with humans and snail-borne schistosomiasis is transmitted.

79 **Bract arrangement in the coconut fruit in relation to attack by the coconut mite *Eriophyes guerreronis* Keifer.**
D. Moore. *Tropical Agriculture*, vol. 63, no. 4 (Oct. 1986), p. 285-88.

The mite *Eriophyes guerreronis* has been a major pest of coconuts in the Caribbean since 1965. Research in St Lucia showed that the arrangement of the bracts of growing coconuts influences the pattern of attack by the mite; the attack was worse where the bract was less tightly adpressed to the nut and where bracts overlapped each other.

This suggests that physical space is of importance in mite infestations indicating that it may be advantageous to select tight adpression when replanting.

80 **Stem injection of vamidothion for control of coconut mite, *Eriophyes guerreronis* Keifer, in St Lucia.**
D. Moore, L. Alexander. *Crop Protection*, vol. 6, no. 5 (1987), p. 329-33.
Injection of the pesticide vamidothion was tested for its ability to control the coconut mite on two coconut estates in St Lucia. The method did not reduce mite damage and yield results fluctuated. It was therefore thought that the method was unlikely to be effective with the old trees present in St Lucia.

81 **Aspects of migration and colonization of the coconut palm by the coconut mite, *Eriophyes guerreronis (Keifer) (Acari: Eriophyidae)*.**
D. Moore, L. Alexander. *Bulletin of Entymological Research*, vol. 77 (1987), p. 641-50.
The coconut mite is a serious pest of coconuts in the Caribbean and in St Lucia losses of copra (the dried coconut kernel) have ranged between eleven and thirty-two per cent over a number of years. Mites were not found in unfertilized flowers but they were present within a few weeks of fertilization, remaining on nuts for up to thirteen months. Increased nut damage appeared to encourage mite migration.

82 **A preliminary investigation of Mankote, St Lucia: a report to the Eastern Caribbean Natural Area Management Program (ECNAMP).**
Allen Smith.   Vieux Fort, St Lucia: Eastern Caribbean Natural Area Management Program, 1982. 2p.
Provides a brief list of invertebrates and fish identified in the Mankote mangrove swamp in St Lucia.

83 **Butterflies and other insects of the Eastern Caribbean.**
P. D. Stiling.   London; Basingstoke, England: Macmillan, 1986. 85p. map.
Provides ninety-six colour photographs with brief descriptions of twelve classes and orders of insects. The study covers an area stretching from Trinidad in the south to the Virgin Islands in the north.

84 **Seashells of the Caribbean.**
Lesley Sutty.   London; Basingstoke, England: Macmillan, 1990. 106p. map. (Macmillan Caribbean Pocket Natural History Series).
This book is beautifully illustrated with colour photographs which illuminate the description of most of the common seashells of the region. Chapters on habitat, reproduction and the development of shells, plus notes on colour, pigmentation, where to collect, local laws relating to shell gathering, preservation and the cleaning of shells provide guidance for the non-specialist, and especially for visitors. A glossary of shell terms and an index of popular and Latin names of shells is also included.

Flora

85 **Typification of *Juniperus barbadensis L.* and *Juniperus bermudiana L.* and rediscovery of *Juniperus barbadensis* from St Lucia, British West Indies.**
Robert P. Adams, C. E. Jarvis, V. Slane, T. A. Zanoni. *Taxonomy*, vol. 36, no. 2 (1987), p. 441-45.
Reports on the rediscovery of *J. barbadensis* on St Lucia, where it should be considered as threatened due to its small population of approximately twenty-five trees that occupy an area of about ten metres by sixty metres.

86 **Forbidden fruit (*Citrus sp. Rutaceae*) rediscovered in St Lucia (West Indies).**
Kim D. Bowman, Frederick G. Gmitter Jr. *Economic Botany*, vol. 44, no. 2 (1990), p. 165-73.
The authors consider three trees which appear to be like those described in early nineteenth-century Caribbean literature as 'forbidden fruit' and which have been found growing in St Lucia. The close relationship between the 'forbidden fruit' and the grapefruit may make this rediscovered species, which was thought to be extinct, an important genetic resource for citrus breeding programmes.

87 **Morphology of dooryard gardens: patterns, imprints and transformations in St Lucia, West Indies.**
Barbara E. Fredrich. PhD thesis, University of California, Los Angeles, California, 1975. 362p. (Available from University Microfilms International, Ann Arbor, Michigan, order no. DA 7608992).
Fredrich bases her study on a year's fieldwork in 1970 and 1971, during which plants were collected from 160 dooryard gardens, mainly in the northern part of the island. Informants were usually female adults. The spatial patterning of plants in gardens and the cultural and historical influences on their usage are examined.

88 **Tropical blossoms of the Caribbean.**
Dorothy and Bob Hargreaves. Portland, Oregon: Hargreaves Industrial, 1960. 65p.
Includes over 100 colour plates with brief descriptions, Latin names and local names in English and Spanish.

89 **Tropical trees found in the Caribbean, South America, Central America and Mexico.**
Dorothy and Bob Hargreaves. Portland, Oregon: Hargreaves Industrial, 1965. 65p.
Aimed at tourists, this guidebook contains over 125 colour plates with brief descriptions of each tree. Latin names and local names in English, French, Spanish and Dutch are also given.

90 **Flowers of the Caribbean.**
G. W. Lennox, S. A. Seddon.   London; Basingstoke, England:
Macmillan, 1978. 72p. (Macmillan Caribbean Pocket Natural History
Series).

Describes the most common flowering plants of the region with the aid of excellent
colour photographs. Aimed at the tourist with little or no botanical training the book is
organized in four parts: herbs; shrubs; trees; and orchids. The introduction describes
the various parts of flowers and their countries of origin. A checklist is provided at the
end of the book.

91 **Trees of the Caribbean.**
S. A. Seddon, G. W. Lennox.   London; Basingstoke, England:
Macmillan, 1980. 74p. (Macmillan Caribbean Pocket Natural History
Series).

Designed to be used by the curious visitor, this book is divided into four sections:
ornamental trees; palms; fruit trees; and coast trees. Each species is illustrated with at
least one photograph and described in terms of size, leaf shape, flowers, fruits and
flowering times in the different islands. A check list is also provided.

**Tourism and marine parks in the sustainable management of coral reefs:
Barbados and St Lucia.**
See item no. 105.

Compte-rendu de la mission à Sainte-Lucie. (Account of the mission to
St Lucia).
See item no. 433.

Tourism and Travel Guides

Social and economic impact

92 **Tourism as a development tool in the West Indian Lesser Antilles.**
David J. Andre, Don R. Hoy. *Caribbean Studies,* vol. 15, no. 1 (April 1975), p. 32-49. map.

The authors discuss the positive and negative affects of tourism on these small islands. Tourist spending in 1969 for St Lucia was US$28 per capita, slightly more than in St Vincent and Dominica but less than ten per cent of the level in Antigua. These funds formed only sixteen per cent of the national income in St Lucia in 1969 compared to eighty-nine per cent in Antigua. There were some negative social and cultural effects which the government of St Lucia was attempting to overcome through 'attitude seminars' with local community leaders and groups to educate the people on the benefits of tourism and its potential for contributing to a better standard of living for all.

93 **St Lucia visitor expenditure and motivational survey (VEMS), summer 1977 and winter 1978 surveys: final report.**
Jane Belfon. Barbados: Caribbean Tourist Research and Development Centre (CTRDC) and Program of Tourism Development (CICATUR/ Barbados) of the Organization of American States (OAS), April 1980. 59p.

Analyses the results of two surveys carried out in 1977-78 to determine the nature of tourists visiting St Lucia. The 2,947 questionnaires which were completed were representative of 5,911 visitors to the island, which made up 8.6 per cent of the total number of visitors for that year. In the summer survey 33.6 per cent of visitors came from the United States, 26.2 per cent from Canada and 20.4 per cent came from the United Kingdom, while in the winter survey the figures were 40.8 per cent, 42.0 per cent and 9.5 per cent respectively. Most visitors travelled in parties of two, saw their destination in terms of sun, sea and beaches and stayed in one of the large foreign-owned hotels. Visitors on package tours spent only half as much on the island as those travelling independently. Over half the visitors were college graduates and earned relatively high incomes. Most complaints focused on local transport (Leeward Island Air Transport, buses and taxis), on services at the airport and hotels, and on unfriendly attitudes towards visitors.

94   **Caribbean tourism statistical report: 1991 edition.**
       Caribbean Tourism Organization.   Christ Church, Barbados: Caribbean
       Tourism Organization, 1992. 203p.

This is the fifteenth in a series of annual publications providing statistical information on tourism in the thirty-two member countries of the Caribbean Tourism Organization. It reports that tourist arrivals increased by 13.2 per cent to reach 159,034 in St Lucia in 1991. Europe, including the United Kingdom, remained the most important market, accounting for just over thirty-six per cent of total arrivals, twenty-one per cent of which came from the United Kingdom. This was followed by the United States with 26.4 per cent. Cruise passenger arrivals grew by a very significant 49.9 per cent to 152,781 in 1991.

95   **An overview of tourism as a major positive force in Caribbean**
       economic growth and development.
       Caribbean Tourism Research and Development Centre.   Christ Church,
       Barbados: CTRDC, 1986. 39p.

This brief study argues that tourism can be a positive force for strengthening the cultural fabric of the region, improving international relations and providing motivation for stability. It reviews the performance of tourism over the period 1970 to 1985 for the twenty-seven members of the Caribbean Tourism Research and Development Centre. Between 1979 and 1982 St Lucia earned US$153 million from tourism compared to US$54.2 million from bananas. Tourism accounted for approximately nineteen per cent of St Lucia's GDP in 1978 and the tourist multiplier was 0.80.

96   **Tourism product development and marketing in St Lucia.**
       Agnes Francis.   In: *Tourism marketing and management in the*
       Caribbean.   Edited by Dennis J. Gayle, Jonathan N. Goodrich.
       London; New York: Routledge, 1993, p. 69-77.

Provides a description of the role of tourism in the island's economy, and of marketing and tourism product development in the early 1990s. In 1990 the St Lucia Tourist Board decided to develop a new ecotourism marketing strategy with the target market being the environmentally conscious visitor because it was increasingly being felt that mass market tourism was having a detrimental effect on socio-cultural and environmental aspects of island life. The environmental aspects of tourism are also discussed in *Tourism and the environment: a case study of the Vieux Fort area (Saint Lucia, West Indies)* (Yves Renard. Port of Spain: Economic Commission for Latin America and the Caribbean [ECLAC], 1985. 105p. maps). The paper, which was given at the Wider Caribbean Expert Meeting on Environment and Tourism in Caribbean Development, links the growth of tourism in the isolated southern tip of St Lucia to the Maria Islands Nature Reserve and the conservation of much of the south-east coast.

97 **From plantation to resort: tourism and dependency in a West Indian island.**
J. A. Friedman.   PhD thesis, the Graduate School, Rutgers University, New Brunswick, New Jersey, 1983. maps. bibliog. (Available from University Microfilms International, Ann Arbor, Michigan, order no. DA 8906368).

Friedman explores the dynamics of tourism-related work in St Lucia, comparing and contrasting wage earners working in foreign-owned resort hotels and petty entrepreneurs involved in various tourist related activities.

98 **Health care tourism in the Caribbean.**
Jonathan N. Goodrich.   In: *Tourism marketing and management in the Caribbean.*   Edited by Dennis J. Gayle, Jonathan N. Goodrich. London; New York: Routledge, 1993, p. 122-28.

Only seven resorts in the Caribbean, of which two are in St Lucia, specifically advertise their health or spa programmes for visitors. A content analysis of tourist brochures and interviews with tourist offices identified the Diamond Mineral Baths and the Le Sport Hotel in St Lucia. The natural steaming spa at the Diamond Mineral Baths is said to be a cure for nervous disorders and hangovers and the main users are young white visitors from the United States. Neither travel agents nor Caribbean tourist offices had heard of health tourism.

99 **The Caribbean: far greater dependence on tourism likely.**
Jean Holder.   *The Courier,* no. 122 (July-Aug. 1990), p. 74-79.

This report by the Secretary-General of the Caribbean Tourism Organisation emphasizes that tourism has become more important to the region during the 1980s as prices for exports of agricultural products, oil and bauxite have fallen. Visitor expenditure in 1988 as a percentage of visible exports was forty-eight per cent for St Lucia, the highest level of all the Windward islands. The problems of land and manpower utilization, utilities, infrastructure, the construction of hotels and marinas and fish resources in relation to tourism are considered.

100 **Report to the Government of St Lucia on the development of handicrafts.**
Charles McGee.   Geneva: International Labour Office, 1969. 38p.

Discusses the fact that tourism is providing a market for craft work in St Lucia but points out that training is needed if quality items are to be produced. McGee reports that the apprenticeship system is unsatisfactory because there is an insufficient number of competent craftsmen available in St Lucia to provide training. He recommends that a handicraft training centre be established to concentrate on woodwork, ceramics and weaving using local materials.

101   **Report on vegetable production and the tourist industry in
St Lucia.**
Janet D. Momsen.   Calgary, Canada: University of Calgary,
Department of Geography, 1972. 81p. maps.

This report is based on a field survey carried out in 1971 of all hotels and guest houses
and a random sample of thirty-five per cent of the vegetable farmers proportionately
distributed throughout the island. It was found that very little of the food used in the
hotels was produced locally. Results also showed that there was a need for irrigation
to overcome the seasonality of vegetable production. Small farmer's produce needed
to be of a more consistent quality and there needed to be a more reliable supply before
hotels would increase their consumption. At the same time hotels had to be prepared
to offer more local dishes to visitors.

102   **Recent changes in Caribbean tourism with special reference to
St Lucia and Montserrat.**
J. Henshall Momsen.   In: *Canadian studies of parks, recreation and
tourism in foreign lands.*   Edited by John S. Marsh.   Peterborough,
Canada: Trent University, Department of Geography, 1986, p. 32-55.
(Occasional Paper, no. 11).

Compares two surveys of tourism and agriculture in St Lucia carried out in 1971 and
1984. Tourist arrivals more than doubled between 1971 and 1984, growing at an
annual rate of eleven per cent between 1970 and 1976, falling to four per cent between
1976 and 1982 and then increasing again to eight per cent by 1984. Although in 1971
fifty-eight per cent of hotels were owned by local people the advent of large,
predominantly British-owned hotels meant that only thirteen per cent of tourist rooms
were in local ownership by 1984. This early British investment and the opening of an
airport capable of taking jumbo jets encouraged the island to cater for European
package tours, especially from Britain, West Germany and Italy. In 1971 the
proportion of food imported for tourist consumption was seventy per cent by value but
by 1984 this had fallen to fifty-eight per cent.

103   **Task force to look at all-inclusives.**
Rod Prince.   *Insight*, vol. 16, no. 9 (Sept. 1993), p. 10.

Eight of St Lucia's major hotels, which account for half of St Lucia's 2,932 rooms,
provide all-inclusive package deals. In this article the author describes how the recent
growth of these resorts has led to a seventy-five per cent fall in business for the
operators of small hotels and restaurants. St Lucia's revenue from tourism in 1992 was
EC$561.2 million, an increase of 20.3 per cent over 1991. Stopover arrivals in the first
six months of 1993 increased by 8.3 per cent over 1992 but cruise ship arrivals fell by
7.8 per cent because of cancellation of some cruise ship visits after St Lucia raised its
cruise passenger tax in 1992.

104   **Quality souvenirs.**
Kathlyn Russell.   *The Caribbean and West Indies Chronicle,* vol. 100,
no. 1,583 (Dec./Jan. 1985), p. 10.

Reports on two St Lucian companies producing high quality souvenirs which are very
popular with tourists both on St Lucia and in neighbouring islands. Bagshaws of St
Lucia, which was founded by a retired American in 1960, produces hand silk-screened

table linen, wall hangings and clothes. It employs about 100 St Lucians, with the sewing carried out under contract, and sells to tourists locally. The second company, Caribelle Batik, is owned by two Englishmen and trains and employs about sixty local workers. It sells its locally inspired batik wall hangings and clothes widely throughout the region using much sea-island cotton from St Kitts.

105 **Tourism and marine parks in the sustainable management of coral reefs: Barbados and St Lucia.**
Judie Snow. MES thesis, York University, Toronto, 1990. bibliog.
Examines ways to prevent tourist damage to coral reef ecosystems through the use of marine parks. Case-studies of Barbados and St Lucia are used to substantiate the argument.

106 **Le tourisme dans les petites antilles anglophones.** (Tourism in the English-speaking Lesser Antilles).
Paul F. Wilkinson. In: *Iles et tourisme en milieux tropical et subtropical* (Islands and tourism in tropical and subtropical environments). Edited by the Centre d'Études de Géographie Tropicale du CNRS, Centre de Recherches Sur les Espaces Tropicaux de l'Université de Bordeaux III et la SEPANRIT. Talence, France: CEGET, 1989, p. 105-24.
A study of recent patterns of tourism in twelve small island states of the Commonwealth Caribbean. Four patterns of tourist flow in the 1980s are examined: fluctuations; fluctuation/growth; steady growth; and dramatic growth. A case-study of St Lucia demonstrates the causes and effects of fluctuations in the tourism sector.

The Caribbean Islands: endless geographical diversity.
See item no. 12.

Travel guides and travellers' accounts

107 **The spell of the Caribbean Islands.**
Archie Bell. New York: Robert M. McBride & Company, 1926. 361p. map. bibliog.
This is the story of a summer voyage by cargo ship through the Lesser Antilles in the early twentieth century. In the chapter on St Lucia, Castries is described as a death trap where 'miasmic vapors arise from the swamp and make the city impossible for white people'. Poisonous snakes and racial friction between East Indians and Afro-Caribbean residents add to the generally negative picture presented here.

108 Orchids on the Calabash Tree.

George T. Eggleston. London; Worcester, Massachusetts: Frederick Muller, 1963. 254p.

In 1956 an American couple, the author and his wife, decided to settle in St Lucia and in this book they provide a detailed description of island life during a period when tourism was just beginning.

109 St Lucia: a supplement to the Caribbean Chronicle.

Guy Ellis. *The Caribbean and West Indies Chronicle*, vol. 99, no. 1,572 (Feb./March 1983), 24p.

The problems that have led to the island's economic malaise and the government's strategy for recovery are described in this series of articles. The government's policies include inducements to attract overseas investment, including an investment treaty with Britain, the improvement of infrastructure and air services, industrialization, diversifying agriculture and expanding tourism.

110 St Lucia: Helen of the West Indies.

G. Ellis. London; Basingstoke, England: Macmillan Caribbean, 1988. 2nd ed. 73p. maps.

The author of this guide book to St Lucia is the editor of the island's local paper, *The Voice*, which is the oldest newspaper in the Eastern Caribbean. Not only does Ellis describe the tourist sights and activities on the island but he also discusses famous St Lucians such as the artist Dunstan St Omer, and the two Nobel Prize winners, the poet Derek Walcott, and the economist Sir Arthur Lewis. There is also a chapter on the recently discovered local hero, Jean Baptiste Bideau who was born in the eastern village of Desruisseaux in 1770. Bideau fought with Simon Bolivar and saved his life during the revolutionary wars in Venezuela where he was killed in 1817. Mention is also made of Josephine Tascher de la Pagerie, who, born shortly before Bideau, in 1763 on her family plantation at Paix Bouche, was to become the wife of Napoleon and Empress of France. Her family left St Lucia in 1771.

111 The traveller's tree: a journey through the Caribbean Islands.

Patrick Leigh Fermor. London: John Murray, 1950. 403p. map.

An illustrated descriptive account of life in the British and French islands of the Caribbean in the immediate post-war period. The section on St Lucia (p. 197-204) describes Soufrière and the nearby sulphur baths, the ceremonies of Speech Day at St Mary's College and the celebration of the feast of St Lucia.

112 The English in the West Indies; or, the bow of Ulysses.

James Anthony Froude. New York: Charles Scribner, 1888. Rev. ed., New York: Negro Universities Press, 1969. 373p.

Froude is an unashamed imperialist and in this account he tells of his visit to the West Indies in 1887. Much of the book is given over to his reflections on the benefits of colonial rule and the subordinate position of the negro. However, he liked St Lucia, which he found 'the most exquisite place which nature had ever made, so perfect were the forms of the forest-clothed hills, the glens dividing them and the high mountain ranges in the interior still draped in the white mist of morning'.

113   **Beautiful Helen of the West Indies.**
George Hunte.   *The Bajan*, vol. 10, no. 11 (July 1963), p. 9-12.

Hunte, also the editor of *The Bajan*, reports on the potential contribution of St Lucia to the newly established Federation of the West Indies. He extols the beauty of the island's landscape and the health-giving qualities of the water and mud from the hot sulphur springs near Soufrière but complains about the state of the roads and the airport. Hunte sees the Federation as being able to assist in the development of St Lucia.

114   **The baths of Absalom: a footnote to Froude.**
James Pope-Hennessy.   London: Allan Wingate Publishers, 1954.
64p.

The author, whose grandfather was Governor of Barbados in the 1870s, narrates the story of his journey by banana boat to spend the winter in Dominica in 1952. The second stop on the voyage was at Castries, the capital city of St Lucia. At first the view from the sea made Pope-Hennessy feel that St Lucia was a perfect antidote to the slummy commercialism of Trinidad and the snobbery of Barbados. On shore, however, he found a crowd consisting predominantly of unemployed rural migrants who had turned to prostitution and begging in order to survive. He describes the rebuilding of Castries after the 1948 fire and the squalor of the shacks surrounding the rebuilt area. Overall the author agrees with Froude in his negative views of the people of St Lucia and Dominica but still feels that Martinique and Guadeloupe are positive examples of European colonialism.

115   **Rain forest and sulphur springs island.**
Keith Spence.   *Country Life* (24 April 1980), p. 1,254-55.

In this travel report on St Lucia Spence describes the island's scenery, architecture, food and drink, patois language and the cost of a visit in the year immediately following independence.

116   **St Lucia 'The Helen of the West Indies'.**
St Lucia Tourist Association.   London; Reading, England; Fakenham, England: Wyman & Sons, [n.d.]. 45p. map.

Published in the late 1920s this early tourist guide includes many quotations lauding the beauty of St Lucia. The guide mentions four hotels in Castries and one in Soufrière and provides information on the main amusements available on the island, tennis and a nine-hole golf course. Visitors are promised that they are unlikely to see poisonous snakes.

117   **The West Indies in 1837.**
James Sturge, Thomas Harvey.   London: Hamilton, Adams & Company, 1837. Reprinted, 1838. 476p. maps.

A good idea of the contents of this work can be gained from its subtitle: 'The journal of a visit to Antigua, Montserrat, Dominica, St Lucia, Barbadoes and Jamaica undertaken for the purpose of ascertaining the actual condition of the negro population of those islands'. The authors were English Quakers and were determined to see the situation of emancipation from slavery and the apprenticeship system for themselves.

118 **The cradle of the deep: an account of a visit to the West Indies.**
Sir Frederick Treves.   London: Smith, Elder & Company, 1913. 378p.
maps.

A readable account of a trip to the West Indies by mail boat from England by a former surgeon to British royalty. Treves, whose narrative is vivid, sometimes racist and quite witty, stresses the historical importance of St Lucia, stating that for centuries it was considered the most important island in the West Indies.

119 **Golden islands of the Caribbean.**
Fred Ward, photographs by Fred Ward, Ted Spiegel.   New York:
Crown Publishers; London: Thomas Nelson & Sons, [n.d.]. 160p.

Ward has divided his account into five sections: the Virgin Islands; the Dutch and French Antilles; Dominica and the Planter Islands; the Windwards; and the Island Nations. Each section has an introduction covering the island's geology and history with many black-and-white historical photographs as well as over 100 colour plates. There are also some nineteenth-century photographs of Morne Fortuné and Canaries plantation and five large colour plates of Soufrière and the tourist beaches.

120 **Love and the Caribbean.**
Alec Waugh.   New York: Farrar, Straus & Giroux, 1959; New York:
Bantam Books, 1965. 310p.

Collected here are a number of travellers' tales of the Caribbean, from Trinidad to Haiti, written between 1928 and 1955. The piece on St Lucia, entitled 'A Creole crooner from the Sugar Islands', is based on two visits: four hours in Castries in 1928 and a two-week stay in 1939. On the second visit the author went to Soufrière by boat and bathed in the sulphur springs. Several place-names are misspelled, such as Fronds (sic) St Jacques.

Prehistory and Archaeology

121 **Petroglyphs recently discovered at Stonefield, Saint-Lucia.**
Robert J. Devaux. In: *Proceedings of the Sixth International
Congress for the Study of Pre-Columbian Cultures of the Lesser
Antilles.* Edited by Ripley P. Bullen. Gainesville, Florida: Florida
State Museum, 1976, p. 213-14.

Reports on the recent discovery of a series of petroglyphs on Stonefield estate, which
were first noted in 1963, although their full import was not realized until 1974.
Consisting of a group of three rocks with eight human figures incised on them, the
petroglyphs are located on the north bank of a dry ravine, about a kilometre from the
coast and two hundred metres above sea level. The main petroglyph is of three human
figures, two large and one small, and matches the petroglyph at Dauphin on the
opposite side of the island.

122 **Rock-cut basins on St Lucia.**
Reverend C. Jesse. *American Antiquity,* vol. 2 (1952), p. 166-68.
map.

Jesse describes thirty-five small basins and nearby petroglyphs carved in rocks near
Micoud on the south-west coast of St Lucia. He speculates that the works are of
Amerindian origin.

123 **The Amerindians in Iouanalao.**
Reverend C. Jesse. *The Journal of the Barbados Museum and
Historical Society,* vol. 27, no. 2 (1960), p. 49-65. map. bibliog.

The author outlines what is known of the Amerindian settlement of the island and
identifies collections of St Lucian Amerindian artefacts. The map shows
archaeological sites of three types: middens; petroglyphs; and rock-cut basins. The
characteristics and discoveries of each site are described in detail.

124   **The Amerindians in St Lucia.**
Reverend C. Jesse.   Castries: The Voice Publishing Company,
St Lucia Archeological and Historical Society, 1960. 25p. maps.

This is an early attempt to provide a comprehensive history of archaeology in St Lucia. Following an outline of the Carib way of life Jesse includes a brief discussion of evidence from middens and petroglyphs found at various sites around the island. Photographs of artefacts are also included.

125   **The Amerindians in St Lucia.**
Reverend C. Jesse.   Castries: The Voice Publishing Company, St
Lucia Archeological and Historical Society, 1968. 2nd ed. 42p. maps.

This second and much enlarged edition contains a foreword by Irving Rouse and appendices by William G. Haag and Professor and Mrs R. P. Bullen. These writers emphasize the argument that the windward coast was the most heavily occupied part of the island in pre-columbian times. A radiocarbon date of AD 450-750 is given for pottery found at Grande Anse and the Bullens provide two stratigraphic tests for the Grande Anse site, indicating linked traits between pottery found at different depths which they identify as Arawak and Carib. They also report on findings from the Lavouette site in the north-east of the island. This edition also contains many new photographs.

History

History of the Caribbean region

126 The Caribbean in transition.
Edited by F. Andic, T. Mathews. Rio Pedras, Puerto Rico: University of Puerto Rico Press, 1965. 353p. bibliog.

Following the period of emancipation in the region the decline of sugar was resisted by planters throughout the Caribbean. Only in St Lucia, among the Windward Islands, was absentee ownership of plantations considered unimportant. Many estates were encumbered by British government loans given to assist in recovery from the 1831 hurricane. No agricultural societies were set up in St Lucia and little attention was paid to improving stock or to the introduction of the plough. There was also dissatisfaction because of the differential between resident and non-resident wage rates for agricultural workers, the large number of IOUs issued and the use of estate shops to enforce debt peonage. These problems exacerbated the flight from estate employment.

127 A post-emancipation history of the West Indies.
Isaac Dookhan. London: Collins, 1975. 191p. (Collins History of the West Indies).

Written for students preparing for the GCE Ordinary Level examinations, this book describes the role of St Lucia in the various attempts to set up a federation in the region. Dookhan points out that St Lucia was the first island to introduce metairie or sharecropping of sugar cane after emancipation but that after 1847 it spread to the other colonies. In addition, St Lucia was second only to Trinidad in introducing a central factory to process the canes of several estates in 1873. Between 1858 and 1893 St Lucia imported 4,354 labourers from India. Also of interest is *Sklaverei, Emanzipation und Freiheit* (Slavery, emancipation and freedom) (Ernestine Kolars. PhD thesis, University of Vienna, Austria, 1985. 638p. bibliog.) which looks at Afro-Caribbean social, economic and cultural history in nineteenth-century St Lucia.

128 **The memoirs of Père Labat, 1693-1705.**
Translated and abridged by John Eaden. London: Frank Cass, 1931.
Reprinted, 1970. 263p.

Constitutes a summary of the eight-volume edition of the *Nouveau voyage aux Isles de l'Amérique*, which was published in Paris in 1743. Père Labat was a French missionary who worked in the West Indies from 1693 to 1705. He visited St Lucia in September 1700 spending two days in the Roseau Valley. He notes that the French settlers from the island withdrew to Martinique during the wars with the British of 1673 and 1688 and so the island's only inhabitants earned a living by building canoes and supplying lumber to passing ships. Labat did some hunting during his stay on the island, killing 'perdrix' and parrots in the thick jungle, and slept ashore in a hammock.

129 **The Caribbean: the genesis of a fragmented nationalism.**
Franklin Knight. New York: Oxford University Press, 1978. 251p.
3 maps. bibliog.

Knight argues that since the sixteenth century the Caribbean has been a dynamic, innovative, pluralistic society where settlers and exploiters, masters and slaves, Africans and Europeans have co-existed because they had to and because each fulfilled reciprocal functions in an almost unique setting of social engineering. The early settlement of St Lucia and the 1734 and 1735 Acts which excluded slaves from trade in cotton and coffee are discussed.

130 **Social and economic problems in the Windward Islands, 1838-1865.**
W. K. Marshall. Cave Hill, Barbados: University of the West Indies, Department of History, [n.d.]. 30p.

Includes two papers, one entitled 'Metayage in the sugar industry of the British Windward Islands, 1838-1865', and the other sharing the title of the publication.

131 **Provision ground and plantation labour in four Windward Islands: competition for resources during slavery.**
Woodville K. Marshall. *Slavery and Abolition*, vol. 12, no. 1 (1991), p. 48-67. bibliog.

The author provides a description and analysis of the provision-ground system in Grenada, St Vincent, Tobago and St Lucia. He explains slave subsistence patterns, internal markets and the quality of the slave diet.

132 **The golden Antilles.**
Timothy Severin. London: Hamish Hamilton, 1970. map. bibliog.

This is an account of four attempts that were made to capture the Spanish possessions in the Caribbean. The British fleet, under the joint leadership of Admiral Penn and General Venables, with Thomas Gage on his last visit to the Antilles, set sail from Barbados on the Cromwellian expedition to attack Hispaniola in 1655. The fleet spent two days in Castries harbour refilling their water casks before sailing northwards to military defeat in Santo Domingo, followed by the capture of Jamaica from the Spanish.

133 **The poor and the powerless: economic policy and change in the Caribbean.**
Clive Y. Thomas.   London: Latin America Bureau, 1988. 396p. map. bibliog.

Looks at the history of economic development in the Caribbean from the viewpoint of the poor and unheard majority. St Lucia is seen in relation to its traditional dependence on agriculture and the new focus on tourism.

History of St Lucia

134 **St Lucia: historical, statistical and descriptive.**
Henry H. Breen.   London: Longman, Brown, Green & Longmans, 1844. Reprinted, London: Frank Cass, 1970. 423p. map. (Cass Library of West Indian Studies).

This is the first major history of St Lucia. It covers the island's physical environment (landscape, flora and fauna, climate, earthquakes, roads, products and harbours), its early history, the revolutionary period, population, religion, agriculture, the judicial system and administration. There was no cultivation on St Lucia until 1651, when tobacco, ginger and cotton were introduced, although they were replaced on the leeward coast in the eighteenth century by coffee and cocoa. The first sugar estate was established in 1765. In 1843 only one-sixteenth of the island was in cultivation and sharecropping was adopted in 1840. Breen felt that the major handicap facing the island was the fact that the population was poorly educated and generally did not speak English. He provides a list of all the island's governors from 1651 to 1844.

135 **St Lucia in the time of Henry Breen.**
John Brown.   *Chronicle of the West India Committee*, vol. 80, no. 1,404 (Jan. 1965), p. 28-30.

The author discusses the state of the Church, crime, and education in St Lucia in the first half of the nineteenth century. He notes that the first Church of England clergyman was not appointed until 1819 and that in 1842 there were only 400 Protestants on the island. Breen remarked on the power of Obeah when he was on the island and the author points out that this is still prevalent in 1965, with people from all walks of life seeking the assistance of the herbal and magical powers of obeah men and women. Marriages and baptisms increased after emancipation but Breen was still not impressed and explained it in terms of a search for respectability. The pattern of crime noted by Breen, with few serious offences and an emphasis on petty larceny and common assault, remained largely undisturbed until the Second World War when the presence of American armed forces on the island brought new influences.

136 **Candid and impartial considerations on the nature of the sugar trade; the comparative importance of the British and French islands in the West-Indies: with the value and consequences of St Lucia and Grenada, truly stated.**
John Campbell. London: R. Baldwin, 1763. 228p. maps.

Discusses the contemporary attitude that prevailed towards St Lucia which held that the island was unhealthy and 'so full of venemous creatures of different sizes, that the French settlers there were never able to stir abroad but in boots'. Nevertheless the French wanted to keep St Lucia because they believed that it contained a rich silver mine. The author considers that exchanging possession of Grenada for St Lucia with the French would be beneficial. The work includes a map of the Caribbee Islands and Guayana.

137 **St Lucia historic sites.**
Robert J. Devaux. Castries: St Lucia National Trust, 1975. 160p. map. bibliog.

Based on the work of the United Nations Development Programme Physical Planning Unit, this work lists ancient and historical monuments, archaeological sites, bridges and buildings of interest, caves, cemeteries, endangered fauna, estate buildings and miscellaneous historical sites. The frequent fires in Castries (1796, 1813, 1927 and 1948) and hurricanes have destroyed many historical sites. The work contains a list of thirty-eight maps of St Lucia, a bibliography on conservation and preservation and a copy of an ordinance dealing with conservation. A folded map showing sites listed is also included.

138 **Pigeon Island National Park: a brief history and guide.**
Robert J. Devaux. Castries: Noah's Arcade, 1979. 24p. map.

Pigeon Island National Park, which stretches over forty acres of land, was officially opened on 23 February 1979 to commemorate St Lucia's independence. The Park was established as a project of the St Lucia National Trust which was itself founded in 1975. Pigeon Island was the site of the first British attempt to settle in St Lucia in 1722. Before that the island had been occupied by Caribs and had been a pirate hideout in the mid-sixteenth century. Admiral Rodney later fortified the island in 1778 and it became a major naval base until 1861 when it was abandoned as a garrison. After being used as a camp for East Indian immigrants from 1878, Pigeon Island became for a short time a quarantine station during a yellow fever epidemic and then in 1909 a whaling station was established there. In 1940 the United States set up a Naval Air base on the island and the leased lands were not returned to the St Lucia government until 1957.

139 **St Lucia and the French Revolution.**
Bertie Harry Easter. Castries: The Voice Publishing Company, 1965. 14p.

Contains the text of the Tom Ferguson Memorial lecture given on 28 April 1965 at the Castries town hall. Easter suggests that the wars of 1789 to 1815 caused St Lucia to sink into a state of devastation from which it had still not recovered. He discusses how slavery was abolished in 1793 by the French republicans and describes how the British soldiers, weakened by yellow fever, had great difficulty in defeating the ex-slave guerrillas and persuading them to return to bondage on the estates.

140   A guide to Morne Fortune (Morne Fortuné), St Lucia.
Bertie Harry Easter.   Castries: St Lucia Archeological and Historical Society, 1966. 26p. maps.

Compiled on the occasion of the visit of Queen Elizabeth and Prince Phillip to the island on 16 February 1966, this guide provides a detailed chronology of the history of the fortifications of Morne Fortuné with information on the graves of Governors and military officers, many of whom died of yellow fever there in the 1820s and 1830s.

141   St Lucia diary of Lt. J. H. Caddy.
Edited by Bertie H. Easter.   Castries: St Lucia Archeological and Historical Society, 1983. 29p. (St Lucia Miscellany, vol. 3).

Lieutenant Caddy was stationed in St Lucia from September 1833 until April 1834. He was born in Quebec in 1801, commissioned in the Royal Artillery in 1825 and served in the West Indies from 1831 to 1837. His diary of his time in St Lucia makes little mention of military duties or of slave emancipation but concentrates on his social activities of shooting, fishing, sailing, dancing, drinking, drawing and playing cards. He does note, however, the bad state of the roads and the prevalence of fevers.

142   Outlines of St Lucia's history.
Reverend C. Jesse.   Castries: St Lucia Archeological and Historical Society, 1964. 2nd ed. 74p. map. bibliog.

Father Jesse dismisses the possibility that Columbus himself could have discovered St Lucia but concludes that it probably was first named by the Spanish as it appears on a Vatican globe of 1520 as Santa Lucia. A dictionary of the Carib language prepared in 1650 called the island Iouanalao which may have meant 'There where the iguana is found'. The following eleven chapters describe the history of the island from the period of pioneer settlers (1605-62), through the years of struggle for ownership, emancipation, the Victorian era, the First and Second World Wars, the great Castries Fire (1948) and five Years of Development (1956-60).Throughout this work the history of the Roman Catholic Church in St Lucia is highlighted.

143   St Lucia: the romance of its place names.
Reverend C. Jesse, preface by the Duc de Castries.   Castries: Government Printery, 1966. 63p. (St Lucia Archeological and Historical Society, Miscellaneous vol. 1).

Bilingualism has led to confusion in the island's place-names, many of which are based on topographic imagery. In this work, Father Jesse suggests that the Lafort de Latour map and *Description* (q.v.) available in St Lucia are copies made by the Colonial Office in 1883 and that they include mistakes in the spelling of place-names. The analysis is based on a study of five eighteenth-century French maps and plans and Latour's *Description*, and of three nineteenth-century English maps of St Lucia.

144 **Early days 1493-1763.**
Reverend C. Jesse.   Castries: Government Printery, 1969. 28p.
(St Lucia Archeological and Historical Society, Miscellaneous vol. 2).

Father Jesse traces the early history of St Lucia from its first mention in the Spanish Royal Cedula of 1511 and a French publication of 1550, in which the island is called Fatigate. He describes how the sixty-seven settlers on their way to Guyana aboard the *Olive Branch*, who landed in St Lucia in 1605 because they were sick after seventeen weeks at sea, formed the first British settlement in the West Indies. Various British and French attempts at colonization culminated in the Treaty of Paris in 1763 which assigned the island to France. The author provides detailed translations of quotations from early documents.

145 **'An equal right to the soil': the rise of a peasantry in St Lucia 1838-1900.**
Michael Louis.   PhD thesis, Johns Hopkins University, Baltimore, Maryland, 1982. bibliog. (Available from University Microfilms International, Ann Arbor, Michigan, order no. DA 8213426).

Louis studies the diverse ways in which the post-emancipation peasantry of St Lucia developed, because of the restrictive measures taken to prevent ex-slaves becoming landowners. The 1849 riots provided an example of collective action taken by peasants against increased land taxes. By the end of the nineteenth century a working-class consciousness had emerged.

146 **St Lucia in the economic history of the Windward Islands: the nineteenth century experience.**
W. K. Marshall.   *Caribbean Quarterly*, vol. 35, no. 3, 1989, p. 25-34.

The author provides an overview of the St Lucian economic performance in the nineteenth century in relation to the other Windward Islands. The extent to which growth and change occurred and the factors which constrained economic development are considered.

147 **St Lucia by a naval officer.**
Naval Officer.   *The Journal of the Royal United Service Institution*, vol. 32, no. 143 (1888), p. 601-07.

Describes the work which was carried out in order to make Castries a fortified naval coaling station serving the Windward Islands. This entailed the construction of wharves, deepening the harbour, removing coral and replacing obsolete defences. The official plan was that the harbour should accommodate 'four first-class men-of-war or Atlantic liners, four vessels of rather more moderate dimensions and a considerable number of small ones'. The work was financed by a sum of £70,000, voted by the St Lucia legislature with no assistance from the Imperial government. The author suggests that the transfer of the bulk of the troops from Barbados to St Lucia would not be welcome to either the troops or to the Barbadians but he considers St Lucia to be more interesting and picturesque although Castries itself is unhealthy and insanitary.

148 **A history of the voyages and travels of Captain N. Uring with new draughts of the Bay of Honduras and the Caribee Islands; and particularly of St Lucia, and the harbour of Petit Carenage into which ships may run in bad weather and be safe from all winds and storms: very useful for Masters of ships that use the Leeward Island trade or Jamaica.**
Nathaniel Uring. London: W. Wilkins for J. Peele, at Locke's Head in Paternoster Row, 1726. 384p. 3 maps.

In the 135-page appendix to this volume there is a description of an expedition to St Lucia in 1722 and of the intended settlement of St Lucia under the direction of the Duke of Montagu. The expedition consisted of 7 ships, 49 officers and 425 indentured servants, with live cattle and frame houses. They moored at Pigeon Island and then sailed down to what is now Castries harbour. The Governor of Martinique threatened to attack the island if the English did not leave within fifteen days and faced by the desertion of some settlers to the French and no support from the Royal Navy, Captain Uring was forced to leave. He concludes with a short description of the island stressing the availability of wood, water, wildfowl and an excellent harbour which would make a good base from which to control the French. Maps of the eastern Caribbean, St Lucia and the Harbour (Castries) are included.

The West Indies: patterns of development, culture and environmental change since 1492.
See item no. 11.

Society and culture in the Caribbean: the British and French Caribbean 1870-1980.
See item no. 171.

Utilization, misuse and development of human resources in the early West Indian colonies from 1492 to 1845.
See item no. 446.

Population

General

149 **Report to the Government of St Lucia.**
UNESCO, Institute of Social and Economic Research, Man and the
Biosphere. Cave Hill, Barbados: University of the West Indies,
Institute of Social and Economic Studies, 1982. 229p. (ISER Studies
on Population, Development and the Environment in the Eastern
Caribbean).

Reports on the high rates of natural increase occurring in St Lucia, which are still a
major determinant of population growth. It is noted that there was thought to be a
serious undercount of the area around Castries in the 1980 Population Census.
Potential migrants in St Lucia planned to go overseas for education or to join family
and did not perceive that migration had any impact on their home country. Their
preferred destination was the United States mainland. The report makes nineteen
recommendations.

Fertility

150 **Mortality, fertility and family planning: Dominica and St Lucia.**
G. Edward Ebanks. Santiago, Chile: Centro Latinoamericano de
Demografía/Canadian International Development Agency, 1985. 123p.

Mortality, fertility and family planning in Dominica and St Lucia for the period 1950
to the early 1980s are examined in this study, which notes that St Lucia's fertility rate
is the highest in the English-speaking Caribbean. Infant mortality rates are higher and
contraceptive use is lower in St Lucia than in Dominica, while Dominica's annual rate
of natural increase has fallen faster than St Lucia's since 1960 despite St Lucia's

higher level of education and living standards. See also *Male attitudes towards family planning: a study of St Lucian men* by Nesha Z. Haniff (New York: International Planned Parenthood Federation, 1989. 82p.).

151 **A study of human fertility in the British Caribbean territories.**
P. H. J. Lampe.   Port of Spain: Guardian Commercial Printery, [n.d.]. 88p.

An overview of fertility based on the 1943 population census of Jamaica and the 1946 censuses of the other British territories. St Lucia is included as part of the Windward Island group. In 1946 St Lucia was second to Grenada in population size and over the period 1921-46 its growth rate of thirty-six per cent was second to that of St Vincent (thirty-nine per cent). The fertility rate for St Lucia was 6.48. There was little evidence of urbanization over this period.

Migration

152 **Migration and rural development in the Caribbean.**
Janet Henshall Momsen.   *Tijdschrift voor Economische en Sociale Geografie*, vol. 77, no. 1 (1986), p. 50-58. bibliog.

The author looks at migration in relation to small farming, considering those return migrants who have turned to farming and farmers who are supported by remittances from overseas. She finds that St Lucian farmers were less likely to depend on remittances than farmers in Montserrat and Nevis but that women on all three islands were more likely to receive money from relatives overseas than were men farmers. St Lucian migrants differed from those from Nevis and Montserrat in that they were more likely to go to Barbados, Cayenne or Quebec than to Britain .

153 **Migration and development in the Caribbean: the unexplored connection.**
Edited by Robert A. Pastore.   Boulder, Colorado; London: Westview Press, 1985. 455p.

The nineteen chapters which constitute this volume cover the positive and negative interaction of migration and development, migration policy and theoretical issues. St Lucia is shown to have lost a substantial number of technically skilled workers through migration. Many St Lucian migrants had previously been unemployed and seventy per cent of them left for economic reasons such as a higher income, education and a better life in general. In 1977, remittances to St Lucia were worth 5.6 per cent of the value of exports and 2.06 per cent of the island's Gross Domestic Product.

154 **Migration and development in the West Indies.**
Edwin P. Reubens.   Mona, Jamaica: University College of the West Indies, Institute of Social and Economic Research, 1961. 84p.

This is an economic and social study of migration as a differential flow among the territories of the West Indies Federation. The free movement of people within the

Federation was a political issue at this time as the larger islands, especially Trinidad, Barbados and Jamaica, were afraid of being swamped by immigrants. Inter-island migration was not of great importance in St Lucia, although the case of St Lucian migrants was unusual in that they mainly came from urban areas. A majority of St Lucian migrants were women and children.

Overseas populations

155   **West Indian ethnicity in Great Britain.**
       D. K. Midgett.   In: *Migration and development*.   Edited by Helen
       Safa, B. M. du Toit.   The Hague: Mouton, 1975, p. 57-81. bibliog.
Describes the migration of St Lucians from a single village, here given the pseudonym of Two Friends, to the Harrow Road in Paddington, London. Of the fifty-nine male migrants who had married since they arrived in London, thirty had married women from the same village. A further twelve married women from elsewhere in St Lucia whilst five wives came from Dominica and only six from elsewhere in the West Indies. Younger people showed a greater propensity to select spouses from outside their village of origin, thus indicating a trend towards the loosening of local bonds.

156   **West Indian migration and adaptation in St Lucia and London.**
       Douglas Kent Midgett.   PhD thesis, University of Illinois at Urbana-
       Champaign, Urbana, Illinois, 1977. bibliog. (Available from University
       Microfilms International, Ann Arbor, Michigan, order no. DA
       7804086).
Field research was undertaken among villagers in Canaries, St Lucia, and among urban migrants from Canaries now resident in London. Their adjustments to life in the city were examined in relation to the areas of social life where national-level institutions impinge and in relation to the employment of social mechanisms of kinship. A final research finding looked at the changing bases of accommodation on the part of young second generation migrants expressed in a shift of identification from the home island community to one based on race.

157   **The force of West Indian island identity in Britain.**
       Ceri Peach.   In: *Geography and ethnic pluralism*.   Edited by Colin
       Clarke, David Ley, Ceri Peach.   London: George Allen & Unwin,
       1984, p. 214-30. maps. bibliog.
Peach uses the data collected by Douglas Midgett (q.v.) about St Lucia in order to illustrate the specificity of chain migration, of residential clustering by island and even by village within London, and the importance of linguistic affinity which is the basis of the strong links between St Lucians and Dominicans.

Language

French Creole

158 Language and society in St Lucia.

Mervin Alleyne. *Caribbean Studies*, vol. 1, no. 1 (April 1961),
p. 1-10.

The continued use of French Creole in both St Lucia and Martinique has helped to maintain the cultural links between the two islands. Creole gained prestige at the time of the French Revolution when it became a means of identification for the colonial settler in his hostility towards the metropole. Today English is the language of social and cultural prestige, yet in 1946 a mere 0.02 per cent of the population spoke only English while 43.4 per cent spoke only Creole. In 1904 thirty-seven out of forty-three Head Teachers on the island came from the English-speaking Caribbean or from Ireland and would not allow children to speak Creole in school. However, some speakers of Creole refuse to accept English/Creole translation in formal situations such as in the law courts or in banks because they do not wish to reveal their ignorance of English. Creole is still the language of abuse, of jokes, complaints, proverbs, folk customs and ceremonies and of intimacy.

159 Language and development: the St Lucia context: final report of a seminar on an orthography for St Lucian Creole (January 29-31, 1980).

Caribbean Research Centre. Castries: Caribbean Research Centre,
St Lucia, and Folk Research Centre, 1981. 12p.

This briefly discusses the role and value of Creole and examines and compares existing orthographic systems in the Francophone Caribbean. It points to the need for rationalizing the available systems for writing St Lucian Creole and includes a plan for outreach and education in the standardized writing system.

160   **St Lucia Creole: a descriptive analysis of its phonology and morpho-syntax.**
Lawrence D. Carrington.   Hamburg, Germany: Buske, 1984. 180p. map. bibliog.

Carrington provides a structuralist analysis and a rich description of the phonology, morphology, morpho-phonemics, syntax and sentence structure of St Lucian Creole. He also includes an introduction and postscript which offer an historical and socio-linguistic context for the study.

161   **The instrumentalization of St Lucian.**
Lawrence D. Carrington.   *International Journal of the Sociology of Language*, vol. 85 (1990), p. 71-80. bibliog.

Despite the fact that English is the official language of St Lucia, French-lexicon Creole is spoken by the majority of St Lucians, especially in rural areas. In this article the efforts to instrumentalize St Lucian Creole are reviewed. The author calls for direct controlled intervention in the language behaviour of the society.

162   **Des îles, des hommes, des langues: essai sur la créolization linguistique et culturelle.** (The islands, the men, the languages: essay on linguistic and cultural creolization.)
Robert Chaudenson.   Paris: L'Harmattan, 1992. 308p. bibliog.

Discusses the theories of linguistic and cultural creolization. The book includes chapters on music, cuisine, folk medicine and oral literature in the Pacific, Louisiana and the French Caribbean, including St Lucia and Dominica.

163   **Political, religious and economic factors affecting language choice in St Lucia.**
David B. Frank.   *International Journal of the Sociology of Language*, vol. 102 (1993), p. 39-56. bibliog.

This study examines attitudes towards the use and acceptability of St Lucian French Creole as well as the influences on Creole in the areas of politics, religion, education, social mobility and economics. The author also discusses historical and recent developments which have bolstered the use of Creole.

164   **Language attitudes in St Lucia.**
Dena Lieberman.   *Journal of Cross-Cultural Psychology*, vol. 6, no. 4 (Dec. 1975), p. 471-81. bibliog.

Three groups of St Lucian students and teachers were questioned about their reactions to taped voices reading passages in both English and Patois. It was found that the Patois version was rated as being significantly wiser than the English version, which was seen as funnier. Attributes of good, wise, confident and hard-working had more positive ratings for the Patois than for the English versions. This underlying positive attitude towards Patois, the native language, contradicts the view commonly expressed by St Lucians that they prefer English.

165 **A handbook for writing Creole.**
P. Louisy, P. Turmel-John. Castries: Research St Lucia Publications, 1983. 11p.

This publication was prepared on the direction of participants of the Second Creole Orthography Workshop between 16 and 19 September, 1982. The pamphlet is intended for popular usage to facilitate the standardization of Creole orthography. The work presents a brief description of the phonetic system and alphabet as well as an extract from a recording of a St Lucian folk tale using the proposed system.

166 **Bilingualism and linguistic change in St Lucia.**
Douglas Midgett. *Anthropological Linguistics*, vol. 12 (1970), p. 158-70. bibliog.

Midgett argues that the relationship of English and Patois as social markers is much like that described for Paraguay, Haiti and Antigua. However, the last two cases involve diglossia, or a division between a standard and a dialect version of the same language, while in the St Lucian and Paraguayan cases the speech communities are bilingual in two distinct languages. Publicly St Lucians decry the use of Patois, while celebrating it with their peers in private conversation. In St Lucia gradual lexical and syntactical alterations occur along a continuum between Patois and English which is similar to the differences found in the Antiguan situation. Young people often have a more limited vocabulary than older people in Patois and mix English words with Patois.

167 **The learning of English negatives by speakers of St Lucian French Creole.**
Hazel Simmonds-McDonald. PhD thesis, Stanford University, Palo Alto, California, 1988. bibliog. (Available from University Microfilms International, Ann Arbor, Michigan, order no. DA 8906747).

A significant number of St Lucian children fail local examinations because of their poor English. This study looked at six Creole speakers and four English vernacular speakers in a rural kindergarten class and found similar speech patterns in both groups.

Rastafarian language

168 **Rastafarian language in St Lucia and Barbados.**
Velma Pollard. *Bulletin of Eastern Caribbean Affairs*, vol. 10, no. 1 (March-April 1984), p. 9-20.

The spread of Rastafari throughout the Eastern Caribbean is seen in terms of a common cultural heritage and contemporary experience of deprivation. The language of the Rastaman is an important part of this culture. Looking first at Jamaican dread talk, the author makes the connection between positive 'ai' words and the 'eye' of the far-seeing adherent. By contrast, negative words often contain the prefix 'blain' or 'blind'. Some of the Jamaican words have changed under the influence of St Lucia Creole.

169   **The speech of the Rastafarians of Jamaica, in the Eastern Caribbean: the case of St Lucia.**
Velma Pollard.   *International Journal of the Sociology of Language*, vol. 85 (1990), p. 81-90. bibliog.

The influence of the speech traits of the Jamaican Rastafari on the speech forms of the Eastern Caribbean provides an example of the uncommon situation of language affecting language where the influence is remote and the means of transmission impersonal. This paper discusses the particular influences of the language of the Rastaman in St Lucia and its incorporation into St Lucian patois.

Society and Social Conditions

General

170 **Guidelines for the conduct of social surveys in the Caribbean.**
Christine Barrow. Cave Hill, Barbados: Institute of Social and
Economic Research, 1983. 117p. bibliog. (Occasional Paper, no. 17).

Barrow offers practical guidance based on surveys conducted in five Eastern
Caribbean territories including St Lucia. She covers questionnaire design, sample
design, the selection and training of co-ordinators, field supervisors and interviewers,
the conduct of interviews, arrangements in the field and coding of data collected.

171 **Society and culture in the Caribbean: the British and French
Caribbean 1870-1980.**
Bridget Brereton. In: *The modern Caribbean.* Edited by Franklin
W. Knight, Colin A. Palmer. Chapel Hill, North Carolina; London:
University of North Carolina Press, 1989, p. 85-110.

The period 1870 to 1930 was a quiet time in the British and French colonies, once the
post-emancipation turbulence had died down. It was followed by a period of
independence and modernization. Race and class relations, economy, society and
culture between 1870 and 1980 are considered. St Lucia is seen as a poor, unhealthy
island, with over 1,000 cases of yaws treated in the single year of 1935, and with the
lowest daily school attendance rate (fifty-seven per cent) in relation to enrolment in
the British West Indies. Yet St Lucia is also considered to be part of a French Creole-
African Catholic cultural complex, which linked it to Martinique, Guadeloupe,
Trinidad, Grenada and Dominica, with the pre-Lenten Carnival and traditional
national songs and dances as part of this culture.

172 **Human maneuver, option-building and trade: an essay on Caribbean social organisation.**
Charles V. Carnegie.   PhD thesis, Johns Hopkins University, Baltimore, Maryland, 1981. maps. bibliog. (Available from University Microfilms International, Ann Arbor, Michigan, order no. DA 8205082).

Carnegie proposes that the concept of 'strategic flexibility' informs social action in the Caribbean and he describes the social and historical contexts of this adaptability in St Lucia, focusing on inter-island trading by women between St Lucia and Barbados. He argues that the rationalization of operations by international shipping lines provides opportunities for small traders, who see this trading as an extension of their local marketing. Most of these speculators are older women, aged over thirty, but Carnegie notes that more young women were moving into the occupation at the time of study. The survey sample was made up of sixteen islanders younger than thirty years of age (four men and twelve women), sixteen aged between thirty and forty-six years of age (two men and fourteen women) and five women aged between forty-six and sixty years.

173 **Report on co-operative development in the countries served by the Caribbean Organization.**
R. C. Gates.   Rome: Food and Agriculture Organization of the United Nations, 1962. 37p. (Report no. 1,493).

Outlines the history of the efforts to introduce co-operatives into the region since the first meeting of the Caribbean Organization in 1951. The lack of middle-class leadership inhibited the growth of the co-operative movement but in some areas Roman Catholic priests and Methodist ministers played this role. St Lucia had one of the oldest co-operative movements in the region but this had become dormant and was in need of new enthusiasm to revive it.

174 **West Indian societies.**
David Lowenthal.   New York; London; Toronto: Oxford University Press, 1972. 385p. map. bibliog. (American Geographical Society Research Series, no. 26).

This is a major study of social structure and ethnic relations, migration and racial and national identity in the Caribbean. The focus is on the Commonwealth Caribbean although comparisons are also made with non-English-speaking territories. St Lucia is mentioned in relation to migration, its pride in its Carib ancestry and the attempts made by educationalists to prevent children from speaking Patois because it was not a recognized language. An earlier article, 'Research note: field study of St Lucia' (Beate R. Salze. *Social and Economic Studies*, vol. 7, no. 4 [1958], p. 238-39), reports on a year's field project in St Lucia. This was designed to provide the basic information required for a comparative analysis of West Indian societies.

175   **The Caribbean: the structure of modern-conservative societies.**
Anthony P. Maingot.   In: *Caribbean visions: ten presidential
addresses of the Caribbean Studies Association.*   Edited by S. B.
Jones-Hendrickson.   Frederiksted, Virgin Islands: Eastern Caribbean
Institute, 1979, p. 90-118. bibliog.

Drawing on case-studies carried out in Trinidad and Tobago and in St Lucia, the
author uses the concept of modern-conservative societies to explain social structures
and processes in the region.

176   **Barbados and St Lucia: a comparative analysis of social and
economic development in two British West Indian islands.**
Coleman Romalis.   PhD thesis, University of Washington, Seattle,
1969. bibliog. (Available from University Microfilms International,
Ann Arbor, Michigan, order no. DA 6922554).

This study compares St Lucia with the neighbouring island of Barbados on a number
of parameters, ranging from colonization and local political organizations to ideology.
Included in the analysis is a treatment of the early administrative, developmental,
educational and religious history of the two islands. Economic and commercial elites
are compared and the relationship between economic and political elites is explored.

Rural

177   **Report on the Inaugural Assembly of the Caribbean Network for
Integrated Rural Development (CNIRD).**
Regina Dumas.   St Augustine, Trinidad and Tobago: University of the
West Indies, 1988. 47p.

Contains a St Lucia Country Report which identifies the main issues for rural
development in the island. These are seen to be the need for more state support, for the
conservation of indigenous technology and for more networking.

178   **Family structure, attitudes and decision-making among Caribbean
peasant farmers in St Lucia, St Vincent and Dominica.**
T. H. Henderson, P. Gomes.   *Agricultural Administration*, vol. 9,
no. 4 (1982), p. 257-65. bibliog.

In a survey of farmers in St Lucia the authors found that ninety-five per cent were
male and that half of them wanted their sons to be farmers as well. They present the
results of their study in this article.

Health and Medicine

General

179 **Predisposition to *Trichuris trichiura* infection in humans.**
D. A. P. Bundy, E. S. Cooper, D. E. Thomson, J. M. Didier, R. M.
Anderson, I. Simmons. *Epidemiological Infections*, vol. 98, no. 1
(1987), p. 65-72.

The distribution of the intestinal parasite, *Trichuris trichiura*, in a village in St Lucia is examined in this piece. The infection intensity of the same-age stratified population was assessed at the initiation of the study and after seventeen months of reinfection following treatment. The authors report that the frequency distribution of worm numbers was similar at both periods of sampling within a broad range of host classes. As such, the study provides firm evidence that individuals are predisposed to heavy (or light) infection.

180 **Traditional treatment and community control of gastrointestinal
helminthiasis in St Lucia, West Indies.**
J. M. Didier, D. A. P. Bundy, H. I. McKenzie. *Transactions of the
Royal Society of Tropical Medicine and Hygiene*, vol. 82 (1988),
p. 303-04.

This article examines the current usage of traditional treatments of gastrointestinal helminthiasis. The study was conducted in two coastal villages, Anse-la-Raye and Dennery. The authors found that the communities there recognized the existence of intestinal worms and that repeated treatment was an established component of indigenous medicine. More importantly, the researchers concluded that ethical pharmaceuticals were a culturally acceptable component of a spectrum of interventions including traditional anthelmintics and symptomatic remedies.

181　**Hypertension in St Lucia: social and cultural dimensions.**
William Wymer Dressler.　PhD thesis, University of Connecticut,
Storrs, Connecticut, 1978. bibliog. (Available from University
Microfilms International, Ann Arbor, Michigan, order no. DA
7913008).

Examines the social and cultural risk factors that contribute to the development of
high blood pressure (hypertension) and to patient adherence to treatment. Fieldwork,
using participant observation and key informant interviewing plus questionnaire
surveys of one hundred forty to forty-nine year olds, was undertaken in a St Lucian
town during 1976 and 1977. It was found that those individuals who aspired to a
lifestyle characterized by the acquisition of material items but who lacked the
necessary economic resources had a high risk of hypertension. Those people with a
wide social support network were less at risk of hypertension.

182　**Arthropod-borne encephalitis viruses in the West Indies: VII: a
serological survey of St Lucia, W. I.**
W. G. Downs, L. Spence.　*West Indian Medical Journal*, vol. 13,
no. 1 (1964), p. 25-32. map.

A total of 261 sera specimens collected from residents of St Lucia in 1958 were
examined for the presence of antibodies to arthropod-borne viruses. Dengue fever
immunity was found to be widespread among donors in their late teens and older. At
the same time, no convincing evidence of the occurrence of the St Louis virus was
found although there was evidence of the infection of the human population of St
Lucia with Mayaro, Eastern, Western and Venezuelan equine encephalitis, the Una or
Manzanilla virus. There was also some indication of a small-scale yellow-fever
outbreak sometime after 1930.

183　**Dooryard medicinal plants of St Lucia.**
Barbara E. Fredrich.　*Yearbook of the Association of Pacific Coast
Geographers*, vol. 40 (1978), p. 65-78. map. bibliog.

With the use of diagrams of three typical gardens, Fredrich describes medicinal plant
usage and their spatial patterns in dooryard gardens. Some 121 medicinal species
representing 55 botanical species were collected on St Lucia but only five common
species were found in more than ten per cent of the gardens. Plants used for the
treatment of colds, fevers, skin afflictions, digestive problems, as abortifacients and to
assist with childbirth, and those used in obeah are listed. Overall, the knowledge of
medicinal plants and their usage seems to be declining.

184　**A prospective St Lucian folk medicine survey.**
Barbara E. Fredrich.　*Social Science and Medicine*, vol. 15D (1981),
p. 435-37. bibliog.

Reports on steps being taken to preserve and further document St Lucian medicinal
plant usage. The Folk Research Programme for the Promotion of Medicinal Herbs has
as its objectives to legitimize and promote the wider knowledge and usage of local
medicinal herbs. In 1979 the Programme collected a listing of some ninety-nine
medicinal herbs in patois. The names in this list are compared to those of the author's
1970 plant collection but only about half could be correlated.

185   **Papers relating to the treatment of anchylostomasia: report by Dr Galgey on the connection between the parasite '*Anchylostoma duodenale*' and pernicious anaemia particularly as it affected the E. Indian labourers in St Lucia.**
Colonial Office.   London: HMSO, 1898. 21p. (West Indian Papers, no. 78).

This publication demonstrates a link between the parasite known as *Anchylostoma duodenale* and pernicious anaemia and reports on the effectiveness of the drug Thymol as a cure. The study is based on patients observed at the Victoria Hospital in Castries (209 in 1892, 277 in 1893 and 272 in 1894), most of whom were East Indians, although the complaint has been diagnosed in people of all races and ages coming from all over the island. The conclusion reached was that the cause of the anaemia was the eating of earth and a failure to wash one hands before eating.

186   **The age of infection with *varicella-zoster* virus in St Lucia, West Indies.**
G. P. Garnett, M. J. Cox, D. A. Bundy, J. M. Didier, J. St Catherine.
Epidemiology and Infection, vol. 110, no. 2 (April 1993), p. 361-72.

Sera from an age-stratified sample of 1,810 people in St Lucia were tested for antibodies against the *varicella-zoster* virus. The results indicated that very few infections occur in childhood, as has also been shown for other tropical countries. This contrasts with the high case rate found amongst children in temperate countries and it is suggested that high ambient temperatures interfere with the transmission of the virus. The pattern of *varicella* incidence observed has important implications for any vaccination policy adopted in tropical countries.

187   **Reinfection with *Ascaris lunbricodes* after chemotherapy: a comparative study in three villages with varying sanitation.**
Fitzroy J. Henry.   *Transactions of the Royal Society of Tropical Medicine and Hygiene*, vol. 82 (1982), p. 460-64.

This study involved 200 pre-school children from three villages with varying sanitation conditions. It reports on the effect of two means of control of intestinal helminths (worms) – chemotherapy and sanitation. Children carrying Ascaris eggs were treated with the drug piperazine. Over a two-year period this procedure was repeated after every six months of natural reinfection. During the six-month intervals, thirty-six per cent of the infected children were not reinfected after treatment; the difference in reinfection rates between villages with and without sanitation was forty-eight per cent. Regression analysis indicated that only sanitation and crowding remained significantly associated with reinfection. Finally, the author discusses the implications for ongoing health care strategies.

188   **Epidemiology and transmission of rotavirus infections and diarrhoea in St Lucia, West Indies.**
F. J. Henry, R. K. Bartholomew.   *West Indian Medical Journal*, vol. 39, no. 4 (Dec. 1990), p. 205-12.

A two-year study of 229 children in three valleys with varying levels of sanitation was undertaken to determine the risk factors and epidemiology of rotavirus infections in St

Lucia. A fourfold increase in complement fixation antibody to rotavirus antigen was used in paired samples as evidence of recent infection. The results showed that forty-eight per cent of infants experienced at least one infection during a two-year period and that seventeen per cent of children were reinfected. Infections occurred within the first months of life and peaked between six and twenty-three months of age. It was found that in each age group the peak infection period coincided with the dry season and that breast feeding children had fewer infections. The incidence of infection was not affected by the degree of sanitation but was related to crowding within the home.

189   **Review of yaws in St Lucia five years after an eradication campaign.**
R. E. M. Lees, A. M. de Bruin.   *West Indian Medical Journal*, vol. 12, no. 2 (1963), p. 98-102.

The incidence of yaws, a disease common among small children in the tropics, in St Lucia over the decade 1954 to 1963 is discussed in this article. During 1957 a campaign to eradicate yaws in the island was undertaken and in the following five years there was a short period of reduced incidence followed by three years of increase. A survey conducted among 1,314 school children in two rural communities revealed an incidence of early yaws of 46 per 1,000 and 13 per 1,000 while the notification rates, for all the communities in these two areas as a whole, were 23.1 per 1,000 and 3.6 per 1,000 respectively.

190   **Skin diseases (bacteria) in school children in St Lucia.**
R. E. M. Lees, A. M. de Bruin.   *West Indian Medical Journal*, vol. 12, no. 4 (1963), p. 265-67.

Reports on a survey of children in urban and rural schools with comparisons of the incidence of each disease between the two groups. In the rural school 641 children were examined and the incidence of skin disease was found to be twenty-seven per cent. In the urban school 598 children had an incidence rate of 17.4 per cent. For skin diseases appearing in both schools the incidence was only higher among the urban children for impetigo. Social, economic and environmental conditions all appear to be implicated in the rural/urban difference.

191   **Bilingualism and cognition of St Lucia disease terms.**
Dena Lieberman, William W. Dressler.   *Medical Anthropology*, vol. 1 (winter 1977), p. 81-110.

The authors use a cognitive mapping technique based on triads to determine the recognition of a set of disease terms from a sample with a wide range of socio-cultural characteristics. Multivariate analysis of the data demonstrated intracultural variation which could be related to language proficiency.

192   **National survey of the prevalence and risk factors of glaucoma in St Lucia, West Indies.**
Roger P. Mason.   *Ophthalmology*, vol. 96 (1989), p. 1,363-68.

The study involved a national survey of 1,679 black individuals aged thirty years and older, a group that appears to be at a higher risk of glaucoma. All subjects were examined for visual acuity, intraocular pressure, and cup/disc irregularities. A total of

520 people were referred, 147 (twenty-eight per cent) of whom were diagnosed with glaucoma.

193 **Occupational safety and health: St Lucia: project findings and recommendations.**
Marcel Robert.   Geneva: United Nations Development Programme/International Labour Organization, 1976. 70p.

Robert includes a description of the existing situation in St Lucia as regards health and safety, stressing the need for training and equipment. A draft Occupational Safety and Health Act for St Lucia is appended.

194 **Sigmoidoscopy in children with chronic mucoid diarrhoea in rural St Lucia.**
S. Venugopal, E. S. Cooper, D. A. P. Bundy, B. Hanchard, J. St Catherine, J. M. Didier.   *Annals of Tropical Paediatry*, vol. 7, no. 2 (1987), p. 104-08.

The authors found that sixty-nine per cent of a group of children with chronic mucoid diarrhoea, patients who would not normally receive treatment in a tertiary health care facility, had endoscopically demonstrable abnormality in the distal bowel. Sigmoidoscopy and punch biopsy of the rectum are safe procedures which can be undertaken in primary health care facilities. The study suggests that such investigations would facilitate elucidation of the aetiology of this form of diarrhoea.

195 **Antibodies to poliomyelitis viruses in St Lucia.**
A. V. Wells.   *West Indian Medical Journal*, vol. 8, no. 3 (1959), p. 161-70. maps.

An investigation into antibodies to the poliomyelitis viruses in St Lucia is described in this article. It was combined with a study of antibodies to indigenous arbor viruses so that sera were taken only from persons who had never been out of the island. Of 227 sera tested, 226 contained antibodies to one or more virus types and 198 were positive for the three known types.

Nutrition

196 **The national food and nutrition survey of St Lucia, 1974.**
The Caribbean Food and Nutrition Institute, The Panamerican Health Organization and the Food and Agriculture Organization of the United Nations.   Kingston: The Caribbean Food and Nutrition Institute, 1974. 55p. map.

A survey of sixty-five randomly selected clusters of seven houses was carried out, covering one per cent of the population. It was found that nine per cent of children under five years of age were underweight, with two per cent severely malnourished. This malnutrition continued through the school years although rural children had a higher level of energy and nutrient intake than urban children. Obesity was found in twenty-eight per cent of adult females but in only three per cent of the men. Anaemia was also widespread and was related to hookworm infestation. This report recommends an improvement in sanitary facilities and general health services, local food production and distribution, and education in the importance of breastfeeding.

197 **A food and nutrition policy for St Lucia with programmes for incorporation into the National Development Plan 1975-1980.**
Caribbean Food and Nutrition Institute.   Kingston: Caribbean Food and Nutrition Institute, January 1975. 47p.

The policy recommendations made in this document are based on a workshop and on research carried out since 1973. Poor distribution of available food results in seventy per cent of all households on the island consuming insufficient food to meet calorific needs while thirty-five per cent are below the needs for protein. Dietary intakes of riboflavin and niacin are also low. About ten per cent of all children under five years of age are significantly underweight and twenty-five per cent of all deaths of children are related to malnutrition and/or gastroenteritis. Anaemia is also a problem especially in pregnant or lactating women who make up six per cent of the population at any one time. The report recommends improvements in health and educational services and more investment in local food production.

198 **Nutritional status of young children in the English-speaking Caribbean.**
Miguel Gueri.   *Cajanus*, vol. 10, no. 5 (1977), p. 267-81.

A profile of the nutritional status of children in the region is provided, based on three categories: weight for age; birthweight; and hospital admissions. Data on St Lucia is included along with that for eleven other Caribbean territories.

199 **Malnutrition: the pattern and prevention in St Lucia.**
Ronald E. M. Lees.   *West Indian Medical Journal*, vol. 13, no. 2 (1964), p. 97-102.

Malnutrition in St Lucia is a disease found in children under three years of age. Some eighty-six per cent of cases occur between the ages of four and twenty-four months with peak incidence being in children aged between ten and fifteen months. A programme to combat malnutrition was begun in December 1962 and after only one year the number of annual deaths had fallen by 42.5 per cent and deaths for the last five months of 1963 were 62 per cent less than for the same period of 1962. The author suggests that this represents the time that has to elapse for public acceptance of such a project. He feels that the free distribution of skimmed milk powder could lead to a rapid reduction in mortality rates although the permanent prevention of malnutrition can only be achieved through education.

Schistosomiasis

200 **Routine focal mollusciciding after chemotherapy to control**
Schistosoma mansoni **in Cul de Sac valley, St Lucia.**
G. Barnish, P. Jordan, R. K. Bartholomew, E. Grist. *Transactions of
the Royal Society of Tropical Medicine and Hygiene*, vol. 76, no. 5
(1982), p. 602-09. bibliog.
Routine focal mollusciciding following chemotherapy to prevent resurgence of the
transmission of *S. mansoni* is studied for the period 1977 to 1981 in the Cul de Sac
valley. Biological and parasitological assessment costs are considered.

201 **An optimal control approach to planning efficient strategies of
schistosomiasis control.**
Abraham Bekele. PhD thesis, University of Maryland, College Park,
Maryland, 1979. bibliog. (Available from University Microfilms
International, Ann Arbor, Michigan, order no. DA 8016332).
This thesis develops analytical models of the costs of control and the pattern of
transmission of the disease schistosomiasis. The empirical model is specific to *S.
mansoni* in St Lucia. The most cost-effective strategy of controlling the disease was
found to be chemotherapy.

202 **Schistosomiasis research in St Lucia.**
Chronicle of the West India Committee, vol. 80, no. 1,413 (Oct. 1965),
p. 545.
Reports on the Rockefeller Foundation's agreement to provide experts and to furnish
equipment and a laboratory for a five-year study of schistosomiasis (Bilharzia) in St
Lucia. The island was selected as the site for the field programme because its whole
population is exposed to the disease and because the territory is sufficiently compact
to study the effects of control measures.

203 **A sociological approach to the control of** *Schistosoma mansoni* **in
St Lucia.**
Peter R. Dalton. *Bulletin of the World Health Organization*, vol. 54,
no. 5 (1976), p. 587-95.
Baseline data concerning contact between humans and water were collected prior to
the introduction of a household water supply. This study found that the number and
duration of contacts with water played an important role in determining the relative
risk of infection by Schistosomiasis and correlated significantly with the number of
infected persons by age. The author suggests that this type of study can contribute to
the formulation of more effective control strategies for *S. mansoni*.

204 **The sugar-bananas shift on St Lucia, West Indies: bilharzia and malaria disease causal links.**
Thomas Walter Helminiak. PhD thesis, University of Wisconsin, Madison, 1972. bibliog. (Available from University Microfilms International, Ann Arbor, Michigan, order no. DA 7213088).

The shift to banana cultivation occurred at the same time as malaria was eradicated and bilharzia (schistosomiasis) spread rapidly through the island (1950-64). Helminiak found that public and private decision-makers responsible for the eradication of malaria and the crop change did not recognize or take into consideration the potential linkage costs between these decisions. Thus it is concluded that their decisions may have been sub-optimal.

205 **Evaluation of an experimental mollusciciding programme to control *Schistosoma mansoni* transmission in St Lucia.**
P. Jordan, G. Barnish, R. K. Bartholomew, E. Grist, J. D. Christie. *Bulletin of the World Health Organisation*, vol. 56, no. 1 (1978), p. 139-46.

It was found that the size and number of colonies of *Biomphalaria glabrata* were reduced after four years of a snail control programme. Surveys of the local population showed that the incidence of new *S. mansoni* infections in children between the ages of nought to ten years old fell from twenty-two per cent to 4.3 per cent while in a comparison area it remained at twenty per cent.

206 **Value of individual household water supplies in the maintenance phase of a schistosomiasis control programme in St Lucia, after chemotherapy.**
P. Jordan, G. O. Unrau, R. K. Bartholomew, J. A. Cook, E. Grist. *Bulletin of the World Health Organisation*, vol. 60, no. 4 (1982), p. 583-88.

Properly maintained individual household water supplies are found to be effective in keeping the transmission of schistosomiasis at a low level during the maintenance phase of a control programme. The incidence, prevalence and intensity of the disease in the various age groups in St Lucia and the maintenance costs of the control programme are outlined in this article.

207 **Schistosomiasis – the St Lucia Project.**
Peter Jordan. Cambridge, England: Cambridge University Press, 1985. 429p. bibliog.

Jordan reports on work carried out between 1966 and 1981 to investigate the efficiency, advantages and disadvantages of different methods of controlling the intestinal form of schistosomiasis, a disease caused by parasitic worms that require freshwater snails as an intermediate host. Projects in three isolated valleys, Cul de Sac, Richefond and Fond St Jacques, were designed to compare the effects of intensive snail control, environmental improvement by providing villages with water and treatment of infected individuals with drugs. Over one hundred scientific papers were published from the project and it became known worldwide. This volume brings together the various stages of the project leading to the successful control of the disease.

208   **Displacement of *Biomphalaria glabrata* by the snail *Thiara***
       ***granifera* in field habitats in St Lucia, West Indies.**
       M. A. Prentice.   *Annals of Tropical Medical Parasitology*, vol. 77,
       no. 1 (1983), p. 51-59.

Field experiments showed that *Thiara granifera* snails were successful in displacing
Biomphalaria glabrata in St Lucia. *T. granifera* could be a major factor in the
suppression of schistosomiasis in the Caribbean but it is unsuitable for universal use
since it is an intermediate host of the parasite, *Peragonimus westermani.*

209   **The management of schistosomiasis.**
       Patricia L. Rosenfield.   Washington, DC: Resources for the Future,
       1979. 136p.

After opening with a detailed overview of the problem of schistosomiasis, the author
develops a methodology for predicting disease levels in a population. The study
stresses the relationships between disease transmission and the human and natural
environment. This model and method is then applied in a major disease control project
in St Lucia. The same model is also used to examine the cost and effectiveness of
schistosomiasis control in St Lucia. Finally, the findings demonstrate how
preventative planning could take place when large-scale water resource projects are
carried out in other areas of the developing world.

210   **Disease and economic development: the impact of parasitic disease**
       in St Lucia.
       Burton A. Wisbrod, Ralph L. Andreano, Robert E. Baldwin, Erwin H.
       Epstein, Allen C. Kelley with the assistance of Thomas W. Helminiak.
       Madison, Wisconsin; London: University of Wisconsin Press, 1973.
       218p. maps. bibliog.

A team of economists and sociologists set out to look at the economic effects of a
single disease upon a specified area. They used an empirical study of schistosomiasis
(bilharzia) in St Lucia to develop an analytical model which could then be used as a
guide for testing the impact of other diseases on the economic performance of
developing countries. The authors found, however, that there was little correlation
between schistosomiasis and economic performance as measured by the labour
market, and demographic and school performance variables in St Lucia. See also
'Parasitic disease and academic performance of schoolchildren' (Erwin H. Epstein,
Burton A. Wisbrod. *Social and Economic Studies*, vol. 23, no. 4 [1974], p. 551-70),
which reports on tests among thirteen and fourteen year olds in forty-five schools in St
Lucia for bilharzia, hookworm, Ascaris, Trichuris and Strongyloides parasites. A
lower proportion than in other surveys tested positive for bilharzia (thirteen per cent)
and it was concluded that parasitic diseases were not significant in explaining
variation in scholastic performance. Another study of school children, 'Bilharziasis in
St Lucia' (M. K. Pannikkar. *Journal of Tropical Medicine and Hygiene* [Oct. 1961], p.
250-55), found that thirty-five per cent were infected with the bilharzia parasite.

Health care tourism in the Caribbean.
See item no. 98.

Women

211 Empirical testimony: the case of the Mabouya Valley in St Lucia.
Vasantha Chase. In: *Caribbean women in agriculture.* FAO
Regional Office for Latin America and the Caribbean. Santiago,
Chile: Food and Agriculture Organisation of the United Nations, 1988,
p. 97-103.

Reports on a sample survey of 155 households out of the population of 810 households, in eight of the twelve communities in the valley. Thirty-six per cent of the sample were female farmers who worked smaller than average sized holdings, of which most were family land. In addition, women tended to own less livestock than male farmers did. Women farmers depended very heavily on family labour and felt constrained by difficulties in obtaining credit and help from the agricultural extension service.

212 Draft report to Caricom Women's Desk on income generating projects for women in three Caribbean states – Jamaica, Dominica, St Lucia.
Choiseul Craft Project. St Lucia: Choiseul Craft Project, 1983. 20p.

The Choiseul Craft Project employs mostly women. This brief report discusses the project, pointing out that the income generated through sales was only ten per cent of the costs.

213 Women in the inter-island trade in agricultural produce in the Eastern Caribbean.
Economic Commission for Latin America and the Caribbean
(ECLAC). Guatemala City: ECLAC, 1988. 33p. maps. bibliog.

Discusses the role of women traffickers in the inter-island trade in agricultural produce in the Windwards Islands. In St Lucia the traffickers' share of this trade amounts to only twenty per cent which is much lower than in the other islands. Furthermore, only about sixty traffickers operate in St Lucia where they mostly own their own farms and are older than other traffickers. A case-study of a St Lucian woman who sells fruit in Barbados is included.

214   **Report on the Round Table on the participation and integration of women in agriculture and rural development in the Caribbean, Castries, 6-10 July, 1987.**
Food and Agriculture Organisation.   Santiago, Chile: FAO, Technical Cooperation Programme, 1987. 125p.

The papers presented at the Round Table are published in item no. 211. This report includes the discussion that took place at this meeting of the Round Table, as well as an assessment of policies and programmes relating to rural women in the Caribbean by N. Shorey-Bryan and a review and analysis of policies affecting rural women by V. Chase. There is also a full presentation of the statements made by Joseph Lawrence, Acting Permanent Secretary in the Ministry of Agriculture, and an address by the Honourable Stephen King, Minister for Community Development, Social Affairs, Sports, Youth and Women's Affairs.

215   **Towards a recognition of the 'invisible' women in agriculture and rural development in St Lucia.**
Rufina G. Jean.   MA Major paper, University of Guelph, School of Rural Planning and Development, Ontario, 1986. 121p. bibliog.

Argues that the introduction of commercial banana production resulted in a sexual division of labour between male export-oriented agriculture and female subsistence and domestic sector production. This situation allows uneconomic banana production to continue.

216   **Hard work, hard choices: a survey of women in St Lucia's export-oriented electronics factories.**
Deirdre Kelly.   Cave Hill, Barbados: University of the West Indies, Institute of Social and Economic Research (Eastern Caribbean), 1987. 127p. bibliog. (Occasional Paper, no. 20).

This study, which was undertaken in 1983, is based on interviews with 111 female workers in four St Lucian electronics firms. By the late 1980s there were seventy firms producing goods for export of which eighteen were foreign owned. The survey found that the median age of the women interviewed was twenty-three and that over half of them were single although most had children to support. Many of the women reported eye and skin problems and headaches which they associated with their work. They also complained of low wages, the expenses of transport and uniforms and the lack of job security.

217   **The economic role of women in small scale agriculture in the Eastern Caribbean – St Lucia.**
Barbara Knudson, Barbara A. Yates.   Barbados: University of the West Indies, Women and Development Unit, 1981. 92p. map.

Reports on a survey of 245 farmers who represented 3.5 per cent of all farmers with less than fifteen acres, distributed through all five agricultural districts on the island. Ninety per cent of the farmers owned less than ten acres with a modal size of one acre, whilst 42.2 per cent farmed family land. On fifty-one per cent of the farms a man was the principal farm worker, on thirteen per cent of the farms it was a woman and on thirty-one per cent the farm was worked jointly. Men were most likely to do the soil preparation, planting and pest control while the main jobs done by women were marketing, storage and weeding. Interestingly, women scored higher than men on literacy and numeracy tests and three-quarters of them thought their roles were changing.

218 Women and the family.
Edited by Joycelin Massiah.   Cave Hill, Barbados: University of the West Indies, Institute of Social and Economic Research, 1982. 162p. bibliog. (Women in the Caribbean Project, vol. 2).

Constitutes a collection of four papers on women and the family looking at the stresses and responsibilities with which women have to cope. The paper by Joycelin Massiah on women who head households includes data on St Lucia. Based on an analysis of the 1970 population census it is shown that forty-one per cent of St Lucian households were headed by women of whom ninety-seven per cent had only a primary school education. This educational level was the lowest in the region after St Vincent. St Lucia also had the lowest proportion of divorced or widowed women.

219 Women's work patterns: a time allocation study of rural families in St Lucia.
Linda Szeto, E. A. Cebotarev.   Guelph, Ontario: University of Guelph, Department of Sociology and Anthropology, 1988. 49p. bibliog.

This is a report on a 1985 survey of women's time use in twenty-three households in Saltibus over a period of four weeks. Women with older daughters who were able to help, spent seventy-one per cent of their time on general maintenance and reproductive tasks, while those without such assistance spent eighty-three per cent of their time on these tasks.

220 Women's work patterns: a time allocation study of rural families in St Lucia.
Linda Szeto, E. A. Cebotarev.   *Canadian Journal of Development Studies*, vol. 11, no. 2 (1990), p. 259-78. bibliog.

The authors have based their study on a purposive sample of twenty households in the village of Saltibus, carried out during 1984 and 1985. Observation of every member of these households allowed a clear picture of the relative importance of women's productive and reproductive work in a rural community. The study highlights the importance of socio-economic status and life course stage in household time allocation. It was found that older women had more leisure time available and were able to spend more time on earning money and working for the community.

221 Caribbean resource kit for women.
Women and Development Unit.   St Michael, Barbados: University of the West Indies, Women and Development Unit; New York: International Women's Tribune Center, 1982. 304p. bibliog.

The 'resource kit' was developed to provide an overview and introduction to the wide range of resources and activities for, by, and about women engaged in development programmes throughout the English-speaking Caribbean. It includes an introduction, profiles of each territory, and sections on health, agriculture, appropriate technology, education and small business, with lists of projects, training and bibliographies. A final section looks at regional organizations and sources of financial and technical assistance. The section on St Lucia provides a range of statistics on women, pointing out that fifty-two per cent of the total population are women and forty-one per cent of households are headed by women. Of these ninety-seven per cent have only a primary education and forty per cent are considered as part of the labour force. There is also a list of fourteen organizations working with and for women in St Lucia.

222 Woman-headed households, the sexual division of labour and agriculture: a case study in St Lucia, West Indies.
Susan M. Watkins. Ottawa: Canadian International Development Agency, 1985. 120p. bibliog.

In order to identify any barriers to the adoption of new agricultural programmes, a study of male- and female-headed households in Saltibus was carried out. It was noted that the gender division of labour was more marked in male-headed households than in female-headed households.

223 Reasons for the neglect of women in agriculture by agricultural extension officers, St Lucia.
Susan M. J. Watkins. MA thesis, University of Guelph, Ontario, 1986. maps. bibliog.

Women make up almost half of the agricultural labour force in St Lucia. In 1971 seventy per cent of women in a rural environment but only forty-five per cent of men, were entirely dependent on agriculture. A survey of thirty-two extension officers revealed two main reasons for their neglect of women farmers: firstly, women are not thought of as clients; and secondly, the selection methods used by the extension agents actively exclude women. In addition, rural residents did not perceive the utility of the extension service.

224 Planning for women in rural development: a source book for the Caribbean.
Edited by Angela Zephirin. Barbados: The Population Council of New York and the Women and Development Unit (WAND) of the University of the West Indies, 1983. 112p. bibliog.

Contains an introduction by Peggy Antrobus, a methodological overview by Kathleen Staudt, five papers on planning, an appendix by Bernard Yankey and three reports on projects in Dominica, Jamaica and St Lucia. The St Lucia report concerns the Black Bay Vegetable Scheme and is written by Beryl Cerasco. The Scheme is located on thirty-two acres near Vieux Fort on either side of the Black Bay River. Eleven farmers, including one woman, were selected and established on site in 1974 but by 1977 only one farmer had made a profit, largely due to poor weather conditions, management and marketing. The Scheme was restructured in 1978 but irrigation and marketing problems remained.

Women

Trade unions and women workers in the Eastern Caribbean.
See item no. 386.

Gender roles in Caribbean agricultural labour.
See item no. 388.

Politics

225 Compton reveals "Libyan Plot".
The Caribbean and West Indies Chronicle, vol. 100, no. 1,577
(Dec./Jan. 1984), p. 36.

Reports on an alleged Libyan plot to establish strong ties with leftist political parties
in the Eastern Caribbean. In St Lucia Prime Minister Compton prevented the departure
of fourteen young St Lucians who had been offered scholarships to study in Libya,
although some of them were reportedly illiterate, because it was thought that they
were to be trained in terrorism. Compton accused the opposition Progressive Labour
Party of St Lucia of accepting US$40,000 from Libya and its leader George Odlum of
making several visits to Libya.

226 St Lucia now an independent nation.
Caribbean Commercial and Industrial Report, vol. 1, no. 1 (March
1979), p. 1.

This article comments on speeches made by Prime Minister John Compton and by
Barbados Premier Adams on the occasion of St Lucia's attainment of independence.

227 . . . . .Of men and politics: the agony of St Lucia.
D. Sinclair DaBreo.   Castries: Commonwealth Publishers
International, 1981. 208p.

DaBreo provides a brief review of St Lucia's political situation, from 1914 to 1979,
followed by a detailed description of the crisis of 1980-81, seen in terms of class,
nationalist and economic conflict.

228 Restoring confidence in St Lucia.
Guy Ellis. *Caribbean and West Indies Chronicle*, vol. 97, no. 1,564
(Oct./Nov. 1981), p. 15, 41.

The author notes that global recession, combined with local hurricane damage and
political instability, have devastated St Lucia's economy over the last year (1980-81).

Efforts were being made by the government to promote the island's tourism and to attract industry but the economic environment was not very helpful.

229 The role of the state in development.
Cheddi Jagan. In: *Rethinking Caribbean development.* Edited by George W. Schulyer, Henry Veltmeyer. Halifax, Nova Scotia: St Mary's University, International Education Centre, 1988, p. 63-74. map. (Issues in International Development Series, no. 2).

In this chapter Caribbean development is considered from a Marxist and Guyanese point of view, which sees CARICOM as part of an imperialist plot to create disunity in the Caribbean. St Lucia is described as a member of a reactionary axis which facilitated the United States invasion of Grenada and imperils the aspirations of Caribbean peoples.

230 St Lucia's turmoil.
Willie James. Castries: Voice Press, [n.d.]. 82p.

Provides a detailed description of the no confidence vote of October 1981 and the accusations of violence and corruption which led to the collapse of the St Lucia Labour Party government and the forced resignation of Prime Minister Winston Cenac. In January 1982 Michael Pilgrim was appointed as the fourth Prime Minister in three years.

231 Louisy on St Lucia.
David Jessop. *The Caribbean and West Indies Chronicle*, vol. 96, no. 1,559 (Dec./Jan. 1981), p. 25.

Jessop discusses the 1981 fight for the premiership between Louisy and Odlum. Prime Minister Alan Louisy then outlines the relationship of his government with those of Trinidad, Grenada and Cuba.

232 Dynamics of the democratic system in small states: the Eastern Caribbean model.
Donald Collin Peters. PhD thesis, University of Massachusetts, Amhurst, Massachusetts, 1991. bibliog. (Available from University Microfilms International, Ann Arbor, order no. DA 9120927).

The governing structure and systems of Antigua, Dominica, Grenada, St Lucia, St Vincent and the Grenadines, St Kitts-Nevis and Montserrat are examined in this thesis. The political system in these islands has a strong level of stability but an equally strong authoritarian governance structure. It is different from the systems in the larger Caribbean territories and is not adequately explained by existing theories. Another work covering a similar area is *Elections and party systems in the Commonwealth Caribbean 1944-1991* (Patrick A. M. Emmanuel. St Michael, Barbados: Caribbean Development Research Services [CADRES], 1992. 111p.) which considers the electoral systems, turnout and the gender of candidates since the introduction of adult suffrage in the region. It includes figures for electoral registration, votes and seats in St Lucia for the period 1951-87 and points out that the turnout of voters in St Lucia peaked in 1974 at eighty-four per cent. Emmanuel also notes that St Lucia has had only five women candidates standing for election, a lower proportion than in the other Windward Islands.

233   **Politics and society in the south-eastern Caribbean.**
       Tony Thorndike.   In: *Society and Politics in the Caribbean.*   Edited
       by Colin Clarke.   Basingstoke, England; London: Macmillan, 1991,
       p. 110-30. bibliog.

This chapter discusses the extent of the popular consensus underlying the political culture of the ten islands stretching from Anguilla to Grenada. This consensus has been shaped by history, economics and the environment. It was discovered that St Lucia had one of the lowest average electoral turnouts in the region at only sixty-one per cent.

Constitution and The Legal System

234 **Progress towards federation, 1938-1956.**
Lloyd Braithwaite. *Social and Economic Studies*, vol. 6, no. 2 (1957),
p. 133-84. bibliog.

Braithwaite reviews the background to the establishment of the Federation of the West
Indies. In 1933 the Commission on Closer Union recommended that the Leeward and
Windward Islands should be linked to form a new colony. The suggestion was rejected
by Grenada but the other territories in the group held a conference in St Lucia to
explore this further. St Lucia was suggested as the site for the new capital and the
conference endorsed the Commission's recommendations for closer union. The idea
was revived in 1946 and St Lucia was again considered as a site for the capital
although Grenada was finally chosen.

235 **Family law in the Commonwealth Caribbean.**
Gloria Cumper, Stephanie Daly. Mona, Jamaica: University of the
West Indies, Extra Mural Studies, [n.d.]. 256p. bibliog.

St Lucia is one of seven Caribbean territories covered in this work. The authors look
at social legislation for the family and child in the Caribbean.

236 **The West Indies Associated States: some aspects of the
constitutional arrangements.**
Urias Forbes. *Social and Economic Studies*, vol. 19, no. 1 (1970),
p. 57-88. bibliog.

It is suggested that the poverty and small size of the islands in question made it
impractical to give them full sovereign status. The social setting of the Eastern
Caribbean will lead to a situation where there is a divergence between the *de jure* and
de facto Westminster-type of constitutional model that has been introduced.

237 **The history and development of the St Lucia Civil Code.**
N. J. O. Liverpool.   Barbados: University of the West Indies, Institute
of Social and Economic Research (Eastern Caribbean), 1977. 41p.
(Occasional Paper, no. 5).

Outlines the history of St Lucia and the process of codification of its laws over the
period 1842-79. The Civil Code of St Lucia was copied almost verbatim from that of
Quebec with minor influences from the Code of Louisiana. Of all the British
territories, only St Lucia, after seventy-six years of uninterrupted British rule,
managed to introduce a Civil Code which was in effect in conflict in many respects
with the laws of the metropole. The adoption of the use of English in the courts in St
Lucia in 1842 was seen as a way to encourage the vernacular use of the language.

238 **Associated Statehood in the Leeward and Windward Islands: a
phase in the transition to independence, 1967-1983.**
Arnold Norman Thomas.   PhD thesis, City University of New York,
New York, 1987. bibliog. (Available from University Microfilms
International, Ann Arbor, Michigan, order no. DA 8801769).

Associated Statehood, which provided the Leeward and Windward Islands with full
control over internal affairs while the United Kingdom retained responsibility for
defence and external affairs, was seen as a phase in the transition to independence.
The main themes of this study are the role of the international system in determining
the status of territories, the plans for West Indian decolonization, the status of
Associated Statehood as a transitional phenomenon and the place of small states in the
global system. The transition to independence was based on the belief that the new
status offered better access to aid and gave small independent states the same status as
large states within the United Nations.

Time for action: the report of the West Indian Commission.
See item no. 8.

Local Government and Administration

239 **Annual administrative reports of the colony of St Lucia for the year 1904.**
Castries: Government Printing Office, 1906. 189p.

Contains reports on magistrates' districts, vital statistics, public works, the gaol, the post office audit (1904-05), Crown Lands and Surveys, land registry, primary schools, hospitals and dispensaries, the treasury, the Savings Bank and Friendly Societies, and the police department. The report states that violence between English and patois-speaking workers was common and that obeah was also practised. Three executions which took place during the year, the first since 1890, are also noted, along with the problem of the emigration of men to Panama and Cayenne, which was causing a severe shortage of labour.

240 **Address by H. H. Gerard Jackson Bryan, C.M.G., O.B.E., M.C., Administrator of St Lucia, on opening the second Legislative Council.**
G. J. Bryan. Castries: Government of St Lucia, 1964. 14p.

In his address the Administrator noted that St Lucia had a new government following elections under a new constitution. He urged the need to move towards a Federation and to eliminate the problem of family land tenure 'which has its roots buried in the distant past' and outlined plans for the release of land held by the United States at Beane Field and Vieux Fort and its intended use for tourism. It was proposed that the hospital at Vieux Fort should be refurbished and roads, harbour and secondary school facilities improved.

241 **Throne speech by H. E. Sir Frederick Clarke K.B., K. St John, on the occasion of the second session of the House of Assembly, 4th January, 1968.**
Sir Frederick Clarke.   Castries: Government of St Lucia, 1968. 8p.

The Governor notes in his speech that the first year of associated status with Britain had gone smoothly and that preparations for full independence had started. Agreement had been reached to set up an Economic Community in the Caribbean and a Caribbean Development Bank. The island was suffering from rapid population growth and housing shortages, and agriculture had been ravaged by Hurricane Beulah. Funding had been provided by the United Kingdom and Canada for the extension of airport runways at Beane Field.

242 **My colonial service in British Guiana, St Lucia, Trinidad, Fiji, Australia, Newfoundland and Hong Kong with interlude.**
Sir G. William Des Voeux.   London: John Murray, 1903. 2 vols.

This account of Sir William's life in the British colonies includes a chapter on St Lucia (Chapter 11, p. 143-284). The author served as Governor of St Lucia from 1869 to 1878 during which time he wrote the Civil Code and the Code of Civil Procedure. His account provides a description of the political and daily life on the island as well as a geographical profile. Des Voeux stresses the need to clean up corruption in the administrative system. He also recalls his attempt to rid the island of poisonous snakes through the introduction of the mongoose. This book provides insights into colonial affairs but is limited in its description of local culture and customs.

243 **Report on the enquiry held into the St Lucia police force in July, 1948.**
Brigadier A. S. Mavrogordato.   Port of Spain: Guardian Commercial Printery, 1948. 20p.

Examines the general discipline and conduct of the St Lucia Police Force prior to, and during the Castries fire of June 1948. It indicates that the general standard of efficiency of the Police Force deteriorated between 1938 and 1948 largely because of the new social conditions it faced, such as political and trade-union unrest, cinemas and 'the bad influence of American citizens from the American Bases', and because of a failure to provide the full complement of officers for the Force. In February 1948 the police were granted a pay increase but this was not made retroactive which led to dissatisfaction and the threat of a strike.

244 **Issues and problems in Caribbean public administration.**
Edited by Selwyn Ryan, Deryck Brown.   Mona, Jamaica: University of the West Indies, Institute of Social and Economic Research, 1992. 374p.

A collection of papers on public administration mainly from the larger islands of the English-speaking Caribbean. A paper by Hunter Francois, the St Lucian ombudsman, states that the public utilities most often complained about are the telephone and electricity services but the question of jurisdiction for settling these complaints has not yet been determined. There is no legislation as to how the ombudsman's reports should be acted upon so he needs to tread delicately.

Foreign Relations

245 **St Lucia's foreign policy and the fall of communism in Eastern Europe and the Soviet Union.**
Cynthia Barrow-Giles. *Caribbean Affairs*, vol. 5, no. 2 (1992), p. 10-17.

St Lucia's foreign policy in the post-cold war era is examined in this article. The author describes the nation's political scene and suggests areas where change is needed.

246 **Caribbean international relations.**
Anthony P. Maingot. In: *The modern Caribbean.* Edited by Franklin W. Knight, Colin A. Palmer. Chapel Hill, North Carolina; London: University of North Carolina Press, 1989, p. 259-91.

Maingot sees Caribbean history in terms of geopolitics, which he examines in three periods: 1933-53; 1954-61; and 1962-80. The changing role of the United States under Presidents Carter and Reagan and the impact of political events in Grenada are also examined. St Lucia is viewed in terms of its membership of a range of international organizations: the Caribbean Common Market (CARICOM); the Caribbean Development Bank (CDB); the European Economic Community through the Lomé Convention; the European Investment Bank (EIB); the International Whaling Commission (IWC); the Non-aligned Movement; the Organization of American States (OAS); the Organization of Eastern Caribbean States (OECS); and the Latin American Economic System (SELA).

247 **St Lucia: widening its relations.**
George Odlum. *The Caribbean and West Indies Chronicle*, vol. 94, no. 1,552 (Oct./Nov. 1979), p. 11.

This article reports on a speech made by George Odlum, St Lucia's Deputy Prime Minister and Minister of Foreign Affairs, to the island's legislature. In it he proposed freedom of movement between St Lucia, Grenada and Dominica and stated that the three islands were seeking firmer integration. He also talked of closer links with Martinique and Guadeloupe, Haiti, Surinam and Cuba.

248   **A study of the impact of the Bishop Government of Grenada upon United States and Caribbean relations.**
Marcos J. Poole.   MA thesis, The American University, Washington, DC, 1982. bibliog. (Available from University Microfilms International, Ann Arbor, Michigan, order no. DA 1332030).

Examines relations between the United States and Grenada since the coup of March 13, 1979 and the effects this has had. When Guyana, Jamaica, St Lucia and Dominica sided with Grenada, regional harmony was disrupted. The conclusion is that Grenada's policies will fuel the growing ideological debate within the Caribbean rendering regional co-operation less effective.

The Caribbean connection.
See item no. 2.

Economy

General

249 **Windward Islands: an economic survey.**
Barclays Bank.   London: Barclays Bank DCO, 1964. 32p. map.
A brief description of the islands, including their history, climate, currency, income tax, communications, tourism and cost of living, precedes detailed reports on the situation in each island. Population figures for 1962 (estimated to be over 90,000) and production and trade figures for the period 1958 to 1963 are provided for St Lucia. Improvements in air services and a new hotel are encouraging an expansion of tourism.

250 **The Windward Islands: an economic survey.**
Barclays Bank.   London: Barclays Bank DCO, 1966. 33p. map.
A general introduction on the history, communications, tourism and external trade of the Windward Islands is followed by sections on each island in the group. Information included on St Lucia covers: the island's population which in 1965 was over 100,000, of whom twenty-five per cent lived in Castries; the former American Air Base in the south of the island, which had just been reactivated to take jet aircraft; and figures for the export of bananas, cocoa and copra for the period 1958 to 1965.

251 **The Windward Islands: an economic survey.**
Barclays Bank.   London: Barclays Bank DCO, 1969. 33p. map.
St Lucia became an Associated State in February 1967 and joined the Caribbean Free Trade Area on 1 July, 1968. This survey details how the production of bananas and copra had increased while cocoa exports had declined since 1963. Fish catches had also improved with the employment of two deep sea trawlers.

252 **Economic survey and projections: St Lucia.**
British Development Division in the Caribbean. Barbados: Ministry
of Overseas Development, British Development Division in the
Caribbean, 1970. 28p.

The major growth factor for St Lucia at this time was tourism, which grew by seventy-eight per cent over the two-year period 1967-69; tourist earnings were expected to rise by thirty-four per cent per year over the period 1970-73. The second growth factor was government capital expenditure, mainly on schools, water supplies, roads, airports and other public works. This activity was estimated to have led to increases in the Gross Domestic Product from WI$39.7 million (£8.3 million) in 1967 to WI$49.1 million (£10.2 million) in 1969 and was projected to rise to WI$67.3 million (£14.0 million) in 1972 at 1970 prices. It was also projected that if construction activity levelled off in 1972, government revenues would decline, but that by 1973 the new large hotels should have boosted tourist occupancy rates so that steady growth would resume.

253 **Economic viability and political integrity of microstates: volume 1 Boolean analysis: volume 2 case studies.**
Sandra Jeanne Claflin-Charlton. PhD thesis, University of Oklahoma, Norman, Oklahoma, 1994. bibliog. (Available from University Microfilms International, Ann Arbor, Michigan, order no. DA 9418455).

The author uses Boolean logic to accommodate qualitative data in a study of developmental issues. The case-studies of six Eastern Caribbean island states and of the Seychelles include St Lucia and provide the justification for the Boolean logic statements created in volume one.

254 **St Lucia: country report.**
The Courier, no. 148 (Nov.-Dec. 1994), p. 21-36.

An overview of the economic situation in St Lucia, illustrated by black-and-white photographs, is followed by an interview with the Prime Minister, John Compton. The banana industry was hard hit in 1994 by severe drought followed by a tropical storm which devastated between sixty and seventy per cent of St Lucia's banana crop. The report explains how this exacerbated the problems caused by the new European Union banana market regulation, the banana grower's strike in 1993 and the fall in the value of sterling. The article concludes with a list of European Union funding to St Lucia between 1976 and 1995. The grand total amount of aid granted to St Lucia under Lomé I to IV was almost thirty-nine million ecus.

255 **Report of the Federal Team to St Lucia, 1960.**
Government of the West Indies. Port of Spain: Government of the
West Indies, 1960. 76p.

The Federal Team went to St Lucia in January 1960 to assist in the Five Year Development Programme. Their report highlights the financial problems which were brought about by the 1948 fire in Castries. It emphasizes the need to increase tax collection and agricultural productivity and to improve human resources through education and skills training.

256 **Economic stability in the mini-states.**
Anthony Hill. In: *The stability of the Caribbean.* Edited by Robert
Moss. London: Institute for the Study of Conflict, 1973, p. 38-50.
bibliog.
Considers whether the small states of the Commonwealth Caribbean are viable as they
move towards independence. Changing trade relations, especially the loss of the
protected British market, and the social tensions brought about by tourism,
particularly the expansion of mass tourism, are destabilizing these countries. St Lucia
with eighty-six per cent of its export earnings relying on bananas is seen as very
vulnerable.

257 **From plantation agriculture to oil storage: economic development
and social transformation.**
Stephen Keefe Koester. PhD thesis, University of Colorado at
Boulder, Colorado, 1986. maps. bibliog. (Available from University
Microfilms International, Ann Arbor, Michigan, order no.
DA 8618968).
Focusing on a rural coastal valley, the consequences of economic transitions on a rural
community and on a group of fishermen are studied. The economic stages begin with
the end of sugar cane cultivation, followed by commercial banana production under
transnational control and conclude with the installation of a petroleum transshipment
terminal. Each of these enterprises used the valley's resources differently and each
had a distinct organization of production. Local households were marginalized. The
conclusion is that economic development did not lead to a qualitative improvement in
the wellbeing of the local community.

258 **The economics of the Organisation of Eastern Caribbean States in
the 1970s.**
Arnold M. McIntyre. Cave Hill, Barbados: University of the West
Indies, Institute of Social and Economic Studies, 1986. 86p. bibliog.
Analyses the economic performance of the states in the Organisation of Eastern
Caribbean States, including St Lucia, throughout the 1970s. The study provides an
overview of the separate economies and describes their external environment,
examining both the international setting and regional economic developments.
McIntyre sees the economic performance of the 1970s as offering policy implications
for the 1980s.

259 **A survey of economic potential and capital needs of the Leeward
Islands, Windward Islands and Barbados.**
Carleen O'Loughlin with statistical appendices by H. O'Neale.
London: HMSO, 1963. 185p. bibliog. (Department of Technical
Co-operation, Overseas Research Publication, no. 5).
Prepared for the constitutional conferences of 1963, this survey contains a chapter on
St Lucia. In this, land tenure, specifically fragmentation and multiple ownership, is
seen as the major barrier to improving the efficiency of peasant agriculture. Tourism
potential is limited by inadequate electricity supplies and a population suffering from
poor education and health services and it is judged that improved roads are needed if

there is to be agricultural expansion. It was projected that St Lucia could achieve viability on the recurrent account by 1970.

260 St Lucia five year development plan: 1966-1970.
Carleen O'Loughlin.   Castries: Government Printing Office, 1966. 106p.

St Lucia was dependent on British aid for both recurrent and capital grants up to 1963. This work provides a description of the economic situation of the island three years later and makes proposals for its future development. Projects for soil conservation, irrigation and feeder roads are put forward and it is suggested that new crops such as paprika and tobacco should be introduced, the production of vegetables and livestock increased and a marketing organization set up. Education remains a problem, with only 23,000 out of 35,000 children between the ages of five and fifteen enrolled in school. Infant mortality has fallen rapidly but ninety per cent of the population still suffers from intestinal parasites.

261 Economic and political change in the Leeward and Windward Islands.
Carleen O'Loughlin.   New Haven, Connecticut; London: Yale University Press, 1968. 260p. maps.

O'Loughlin considers the problems of economic development in the small islands of the Eastern Caribbean. She explains that for St Lucia social problems are more urgent than economic problems with a revision of the land tenure system, higher spending on health and education services and slum clearance needed. In contrast, St Lucia, which had been one of the poorer areas of the West Indies, is now seen as the strongest financially. When Castries was an important coaling station for ships en route through the Panama Canal it was the seventh largest port of entry in the world. The author predicts that the boom brought about by the banana industry, plus a growing tourist industry, combined with good financial management could provide the basis for a more diversified economic structure.

262 The economy of St Lucia.
H. W. O'Neale.   *Social and Economic Studies*, vol. 13, no. 4 (Dec. 1964), p. 440-70.

Represents an extensive overview of the economy of St Lucia in the early 1960s. The author discusses the country's prospects for the immediate future and points to the need for diversification of both industry and agriculture. The study also calls for increased promotion of tourism through publicity and improved services.

263 Report of activities of the O. E. C. S. Economic Affairs Secretariat, 1984.
Organisation of Eastern Caribbean States.   Antigua and Barbuda: OECS Printery, 1984. 51p.

This is the first report of the Economic Affairs Secretariat. The Organisation of Eastern Caribbean States was established in 1981 with the signing on 18 June of the Treaty of Basseterre in St Kitts by representatives of the seven governments of the Windward and Leeward Islands. The OECS is based on a blending of national sovereignties in areas of activities in which a collective strength is found necessary.

For example, it undertakes the training of middle management in the civil services of member nations, has established an Eastern Caribbean Central Bank, allocates industries to specific states and prepares informational papers and regional statistics. The Headquarters of the OECS is in St Lucia.

264 **Report of the Tripartite Economic Survey of the Eastern Caribbean January-April 1966.**
J. R. Sargent for the Ministry of Overseas Development. London: HMSO, 1967. 279p.

St Lucia is one of only two islands in the Eastern Caribbean region for which a shortage of agricultural land does not restrain development. This report concentrates on identifying the obstacles to economic growth in the islands, the policies required to overcome them and the priorities for expenditure. Coffee and cocoa production are shown to be declining and the need to encourage domestic agriculture is outlined. Land tenure reform, soil conservation, irrigation, agricultural credit, marketing, forestry and fishing are all seen as needing support. In contrast, visitors and the number of hotel beds doubled between 1961 and 1965 and the report envisages further rapid expansion. The potential of geothermal power is also stressed and 'industrial development should be encouraged to the maximum'. The main constraints on development were seen to be human resources since thirty per cent of the population was illiterate and health standards were among the lowest in the region with over half the people without a source of safe drinking water.

265 **Economic development in the Eastern Caribbean Islands: St Lucia.**
Alice Shurcliff, J. F. Wellemeyer. Barbados: University of the West Indies, Institute of Social and Economic Research, 1967. 30p. (Manpower Surveys, Series no. 4).

Presents an analysis of the population structure suggesting that St Lucians have long been the most mobile people in the Windward Islands, migrating to England, Canada, the United States, other Caribbean islands and to South America.

266 **Grassroots development in the Eastern Caribbean.**
Aaron L. Schneider. In: *Canadian-Caribbean relations: aspects of a relationship.* Edited by Brian Douglas Tennyson. Sydney, Nova Scotia: University College of Cape Breton, Centre of International Studies, 1990, p. 173-255.

The author examines specific economic and social development projects in Grenada, Dominica, and St Lucia. He concludes that grass roots projects are the most effective means of self-help development.

267 **Guidelines for the evaluation of transshipment opportunities: the case of St Lucia.**
United Nations Economic Commission for Latin America. New York: ECLA, 1984. 32p.

Reports on the feasibility of setting up transshipment centres at Castries and Vieux Fort. It is noted that although most imports arrive in containers, the containers are returned empty. Expansion of the port of Castries is limited by a shortage of space for port-related activities and in Vieux Fort the local topography makes expansion of storage facilities difficult. Two shipping lines had expressed interest in using Castries for transshipment and marine repair facilities are seen as a possible development.

268   St Lucia ready for take-off?
West Indies Chronicle, vol. 86, no. 1,483 (Aug. 1971), p. 347.

Notes the arrival of the first BOAC (now British Airways) VC10 at the new Hewanorra International Airport near Vieux Fort. The new runway was a gift from Canada. It is pointed out that a hotel of 250 rooms with conference facilities has also opened near the airport and with road improvements and other new hotels, tourism is expanding rapidly. St Lucia has one of the highest rates of growth of Gross National Product in the region.

269   Full speed ahead for St Lucia.
West Indies Chronicle, vol. 87, no. 1,491 (April 1972), p. 151.

The progress of the economy of St Lucia between 1969 and 1972 is reported on in this piece. The depression in the banana industry which was largely due to drought conditions was to a great extent offset by the rapid expansion of the tourist industry and related construction. However, inflation has increased and infrastructure needs expansion and repair.

270   St Lucia: economic performance and prospects.
World Bank.   Washington, DC: World Bank, 1985. 99p. folding map.

A World Bank country study which reviews the current economic conditions, public finance, public investments and infrastructure of St Lucia.

271   Caribbean countries: economic situation, regional issues, and capital flows.
World Bank.   Washington, DC: World Bank, 1988. 78p. map. (World Bank Country Study).

Provides an overview of the progress and outlook of fifteen countries of the Caribbean which is related to macroeconomic policy and sectorial issues. The report on St Lucia, (p. 55-57) notes that Gross Domestic Product growth had accelerated to six per cent a year in 1985-86 but slowed down in 1987 because of drought. The increase was mainly due to higher banana production and to an expansion of tourism and construction but it had little impact on unemployment which was estimated at over twenty per cent of the labour force. It was recommended that domestic savings should be continued at the present level, that agriculture should be diversified, hotel capacity increased and manufacturing provided with more investment and skilled manpower.

272   A survey of the literature on income distribution and the fulfillment of basic needs in the Caribbean region.
Clarence Zuvekas Jr.   Washington, DC: United States Department of Agriculture, 1978. 64p.

The author reviews data collected for the Commonwealth countries of the Eastern Caribbean on income and standard of living indicators using the 1960 and 1970 censuses and detailed small farmer surveys. St Lucia is distinguished by having more medium-sized farms (twenty-five to one-hundred acres) but fewer household heads with five or more years of schooling than elsewhere in the region (37.4 per cent in St Lucia compared to between seventy-seven and eighty-nine per cent). Houses in St Lucia had fewer rooms (2.7) and rural housing had very few facilities. Both male and female life expectancy was lower than in other islands.

Restoring confidence in St Lucia.
See item no. 228.

Sir W. Arthur Lewis

273 **The early education of a Nobel Laureate in the West Indies.**
Solomon Agyemang. *Bulletin of Eastern Caribbean Affairs,* vol. 18, no. 1 (1993), p. 49-57.
An address delivered at a memorial service marking the first anniversary of the death of Sir William Arthur Lewis. The speaker presents a summary of Lewis' achievements and ideas.

274 **The people will decide.**
Sir Arthur Lewis. *The Caribbean and West Indies Chronicle,* vol. 100, no. 1,586 (June/July 1985), p. 4.
Sir Arthur Lewis, Nobel Prize winner for Economics and first President of the Caribbean Development Bank, in a speech at a public meeting in St Lucia, suggests that the future for the islands of the Caribbean depends on the ability of the people to grasp economic realities. He points out that the islands have to live by trade and that their success will depend on the control of population growth and on upgrading people's skills and their confidence in the future.

275 **Eulogy for Sir William Arthur Lewis: given at the state funeral for Sir William Arthur.**
Vaughan A. Lewis. *Social and Economic Studies*, vol. 40, no. 3 (1991), p. 5-15.
This eulogy by his nephew describes the life and achievements of Nobel Laureate economist Sir Arthur Lewis.

276 **W. Arthur Lewis: another view.**
Rex Nettleford. *21st Century Policy Review*, vol. 2, no. 102 (spring 1994), p. 313-35.
Constitutes the text of a talk given at the Sir Arthur Lewis Community College, The Morne, Castries, on January 22 1993 during Nobel Laureate Week in St Lucia. The focus is on Sir Arthur's attitudes towards education for West Indians and the role of the University of the West Indies. Nettleford draws on the writings of Lewis' fellow

Nobel Laureate, Derek Walcott, to explain their leadership in terms of their use of the dialectics of the pluralist realities of their native West Indies.

277 **Sir Arthur Lewis: an economic and political portrait.**
Edited by Ralph Premdas, Eric St Cyr.   Mona, Jamaica: University of the West Indies, Institute of Social and Economic Research, 1991. 125p. (Regional Programme in Monetary Studies).

The first of the seven contributions in this work is an introduction by the editors to the life of Sir Arthur Lewis, who was born in St Lucia, became an Island Scholar at the age of seventeen, Professor of economics at Manchester University by the age of thirty-three, and was awarded the Nobel Prize for Economics. This review of the life and works of Sir Arthur is followed by three essays which critique his models of development with unlimited supplies of labour, export-led development and Haitian development, and three which consider his political contributions to the Moyne Commission and the development of a middle class ideology.

Labour in the West Indies: the birth of a workers movement.
See item no. 387.

Finance, Banking and Trade

278 **Inflation in the Caribbean.**
Edited by Compton Bourne.   Mona, Jamaica: University of the West
Indies, Institute of Social and Economic Studies, 1977. 166p.
This collection of papers on inflation in the Commonwealth Caribbean in the early
1970s includes a paper by Errol N. Allen on inflation in the Eastern Caribbean
currency area. Allen provides tables of retail price indices and economic growth rates
between 1971 and 1975 for St Lucia and six other Eastern Caribbean territories. He
concludes that price increases on imported items had a significant effect on the rise of
the retail price index during this period.

279 **Intra-Caribbean trade statistics: statistiques du commerce
intercaraïbe.**
Central Secretariat.   Hato Rey, Puerto Rico: Caribbean Organization,
1964. 359p.
This volume, which is published in both English and French, notes that intra-regional
trade only amounts to four per cent of the total trade of the Caribbean region because
of customs barriers and the lack of marketing information. The statistics in the volume
are presented in order to provide a basis for research to improve the trade situation.
The data is for the latest calendar year, which in general is 1962, apart from St Lucia,
for which no detailed up-to-date information was available.

280 **Financial and actuarial study of the national provident fund and
the proposed social security scheme.**
Charles E. Clarke.   Geneva: United Nations Development
Project/International Labour Organisation, 1976. 33p.
The first chapter of this study offers a review of the operation of the existing national
provident fund. The rest of the report outlines proposals for a social security scheme
covering financial organization and levels of benefit, pensions and contributions.

281 **The friendly societies in St Lucia and St Vincent.**
Leonard P. Fletcher. *Caribbean Studies*, vol. 18, nos. 3-4 (Oct. 1978/Jan. 1979), p. 89-114.

Friendly societies are voluntary associations established to provide mutual aid to members in times of financial need and for accumulating short-term savings for periodic distribution to members. St Lucia's first Friendly Society Act was passed in 1896 and before 1901 the island had six such societies. By 1937 the number had grown to eighty-eight societies with a total of 8,643 members and although by 1967 the number of societies had fallen to eighty-four the membership had risen to 19,805. From 1968 a central Registry was in operation and the Registrar reported that Friendly Societies were losing popularity in the face of competition from insurance companies and had a high rate of failure. A detailed account is given of the working of St Lucia's largest Friendly Society, the Olive Branch, which was founded in 1921.

282 **The Canada-St Lucia comprehensive project.**
Emma Hippolyte, David Rattray. *International Journal of Government Auditing,* vol. 14, no. 1 (Jan. 1987), p. 12-14, 24.

The colonial financial administration system of St Lucia came under severe stress in the 1970s and changes were made in the financial management capacity of the government. The Canadian International Development Agency (CIDA) was asked in 1983 to initiate a project to upgrade the function and office of the Director of Audit and legislation introduced in 1987 provides for the increased independence of the Audit Department, complete access and full comprehensive auditing powers. The CIDA project had to meet challenges involving staff education and experience, methodology and terminology, audit independence, computerization and general facilities. The authors consider all these factors in this article.

283 **Agricultural credit in the Caribbean.**
Ramon Colon-Torres. *Caribbean Economic Review*, vol. 4, nos. 1-2 (Dec. 1952), p. 60-112.

Presents an account of the history of agricultural credit in the Caribbean. Banks and Life Assurance Societies were the main sources of agricultural credit in St Lucia. In 1940 the Peasants' (Loans) Ordinance was approved for the purpose of granting loans not exceeding twenty pounds each to peasant owners or those with life tenancies. In 1946 a Co-operative Societies Ordinance also had among its provisions that of raising credit from private and government sources for its members. Government credit was available under the Vieux-Fort Agricultural Development Scheme. Agricultural credit was needed to enable the cultivation of undeveloped land and the Agricultural Superintendant suggested that an Agricultural Bank should be set up in order to stimulate agricultural development, regardless of the size of holding.

284 **The growth of non-traditional exports in the Caribbean.**
Philip Williams. *The Courier,* no. 127 (May-June 1991), p. 84-90.

This article notes that industrial development in St Lucia was based on incentive legislation aimed at attracting foreign-owned and managed enterprises. In Dominica and St Lucia primary commodity exports comprised between fifty-four per cent and fifty-seven per cent of total merchandise exports in the 1980s which was less than in most Caribbean countries but more than in Barbados.

Human maneuver, option-building and trade: an essay on Caribbean social organisation.
See item no. 172.

Women in the inter-island trade in agricultural produce in the Eastern Caribbean.
See item no. 213.

Industry

285 Heineken opt for St Lucia.
Castries correspondent. *The West Indies Chronicle*, vol. 88, no. 1,507 (Aug. 1973), p. 324.

Announces the building of a brewery in Vieux Fort by the Dutch company Heineken. The brewery was the second major plant in the island's programme of industrialization. The government of St Lucia and the people of the island took up twenty-five per cent of the shares in the brewery and twenty-four per cent were offered to the other three Windward Islands.

286 Secondary agrobased industries: ECCM and Barbados.
Jeffrey Dellimore, Judy Whitehead. Mona, Jamaica: University of the West Indies, Institute of Social and Economic Research, 1984. 296p. bibliog. (Caribbean Technology Policy Studies Project Series).

The problem of regional dependence on imported foodstuffs is investigated through studies of production and consumption patterns in Barbados, St Kitts, Antigua, Montserrat and St Lucia. Complementary data are assembled from various territorial censuses and household budgetary surveys and a content analysis of advertisements in local newspapers is included as well, as a way of examining the manipulation of local tastes.

287 St Lucia industrial development.
National Development Corporation. Castries: National Development Corporation, 1973. 43p. map.

Provides statistical tables on the GDP, per capita income, exports, visitors and imports for the period 1967 to 1973. The report is aimed at potential investors and gives a description of the island and of St Lucian labour laws, industrial relations, industrial sites and new industrial estates, the supply of utilities, transport facilities, development incentives, income tax laws and customs duties.

288 **St Lucia: advantages for industrial development.**
National Development Corporation.   Castries: National Development
Corporation, 1976. 41p. map.
Provides an updated version of the 1973 publication (item no. 287) with information
current in May 1976.

289 **Free zone planned for Vieux Fort.**
Rod Prince.   *Insight*, vol. 16, no. 7 (July 1993), p. 10.
Reports on the opening of a new deep-water container port at Vieux Fort, costing
EC$40 million, and discusses the new facilities developed at the nearby Hewanorra
airport which cost EC$54 million. This southern tip of the island is now seen as a new
economic frontier, with Vieux Fort predicted to become a major transshipment centre.
The Prime Minister announced a plan to establish a free zone at Vieux Fort, a marina
and a 350-room hotel. Development of the area as the island's major export
manufacturing centre has reduced the over-use of the hilly trans-island road from
Castries by container lorries.

290 **Small scale entrepreneurship in the Commonwealth Caribbean:
the case of St Lucia.**
Patrick Joseph Marius Sylvester.   PhD thesis, Bryn Mawr College,
Bryn Mawr, Pennsylvania, 1973. bibliog. (Available from University
Microfilms International, Ann Arbor, Michigan, order no. DA
7411426).
Sylvester interviewed seventy-nine small-scale trade and manufacturing entrepreneurs
to find out their background and the institutional environment in which they operated.
It was found that the entrepreneurs were handicapped by a lack of working and long-
term capital, largely because the banks were very hidebound about loan policies.
Interviewees also complained about labour problems resulting in very low work effort.

Quality souvenirs.
See item no. 104.

**Hard work, hard choices: a survey of women in St Lucia's export-
oriented electronics factories.**
See item no. 216.

Agriculture and Fishing

General

291 **St Lucia: Hurricane Allan Agricultural Rehabilitation/Development Programme.**
Agriculture Ministry.   Castries: Ministry of Agriculture, Lands, Fisheries, Cooperatives and Labour, 1980. 51p.

Describes the existing resource endowment of St Lucia and its agriculture before Hurricane Allen and considers the extent and cost of the damage it caused to agriculture. There was severe damage to bananas and tree crops and some fifty fishing boats were damaged and another forty lost. The total net income loss to the economy over the period 1980-86 until full recovery is achieved is estimated at EC$11.7million, while short-term rehabilitation projects are estimated at costing EC$45 million. A list of thirty-two proposed long-term agricultural development projects for which funding is requested is also included.

292 **The agricultural and economic resources of St Lucia.**
A. J. Brooks.   Trinidad: Imperial Department of Agriculture, 1916. 42p. (Pamphlet Series, no. 81).

Brooks provides a general description of St Lucia, covering the island's history, geology and health in detail. At the time the government of St Lucia had agreed to sell Crown Lands in lots of not less than 100 acres for the settlement of persons who had recently served in the armed forces or came from outside the colony. Land was sold at fifteen shillings per acre for areas of less than 100 acres or ten shillings per acre for lots above that size. The Agricultural Department was to supply economic plants, free of charge, for planting up to fifty acres. The peak of agricultural output had occurred in 1875 and although sugar was still the main crop, limes had been introduced in 1902. With the decline in sugar cane, plantations beaome more interested in cacao which had previously been grown only by peasants.

293 **Farming systems research in the Eastern Caribbean: an attempt at analyzing intra-household dynamics.**
Vasantha Chase. In: *Gender issues in farming systems research and extension.* Edited by Susan V. Poats, Marianne Schmink, Anita Spring. Boulder, Colorado; London: Westview Press, 1988, p. 171-82. bibliog.

The author describes the work of the Caribbean Agricultural Research and Development Institute (CARDI) which was established in 1975 to serve the agricultural research needs of the twelve member countries of the English-speaking Caribbean. She finds that women farmers receive less income and less attention from the extension service than do male farmers. Men usually make decisions about export crops while in general, women make decisions about crops for home consumption or domestic sale. The Mabouya Valley was studied because it is an area of male outmigration and represents a wide range of farming systems. Women farmers, who form thirty-eight per cent of the sample, were found to depend more heavily than men on family labour.

294 **Agricultural progress in St Lucia.**
Edward L. Cozier. *New Commonwealth,* vol. 32, no. 2 (July 23 1956), p. 73-74.

This is an optimistic report on St Lucian agriculture and the prospects for improvement through scientific advances. Cozier notes the need for the island to break away from its pattern of economic dependency. He also calls for an improvement in the 'semi-productive' land committed to shifting peasant cultivation and points out the need for greater capital input to increase production of sugar cane, cacao, beef, coffee and the emerging banana sector.

295 **West India Royal Commission Report on Agriculture, Fisheries, Forestry and Veterinary Matters.**
F. L. Engledow for the Colonial Office. London: HMSO, 1945. 235p. (Cmnd. 6608).

Despite the fact that this Report of the West India Royal Commission (1938-39) was published in 1945, the data has a cut-off of 1937, because of the delay caused by the Second World War. Food supply, land ownership and use, peasant and estate agriculture, land settlement, soil erosion and fertility are all covered in the report, as well as cash and export crops, agricultural marketing, credit, education, research, policy and organization and forestry. Veterinary matters and fisheries are also discussed. It was recommended that parts of some estates should be acquired by the Government for land settlements. The proposed settlement of Barbadian cane farmers in St Lucia could only succeed if St Lucia's sugar quota were to be increased. In addition, the expansion of the banana industry in St Lucia was making the problem of soil erosion on steep hillslopes more urgent and so it was felt that land above 800 feet should not be cultivated.

296 **Agricultural development in the Eastern Caribbean: a survey.**
Donald R. Fiester, William Baucom, Alphonse Chable, Clarence
Zuvekas Jr. Washington, DC: US AID, 1977. 289p.

The first part of this survey presents a general macroeconomic overview of the region
and the problems of agricultural development. In the section on St Lucia it is
estimated that the per capita Gross National Product in 1976 was US$430.
Unemployment was 9.1 per cent in 1970 and was thought to have increased since then.
The main occupation of islanders was agriculture, employing 33,000 people, but light
manufacturing, tourism and the construction of the oil terminal were providing new
opportunities. The average land holding in 1973 was 6.9 acres of which four acres
were cropped; this represented more land per farmer than in Grenada or St Vincent.
Funding was requested for rural infrastructure in order to reduce rural-urban migration
and for irrigation projects for small farms.

297 **Reports on the Botanic Station, Agricultural School and
Experimental Plots, St Lucia 1906-7.**
Imperial Commissioner. Barbados: Imperial Commissioner of
Agriculture for the West Indies, 1907. 30p.

Notes that the cultivation of the 'Chinese or Dwarf banana' (*Musa Cavendishii*) had been
successful for a number of years and states that the acreage could be increased to fifty
acres within just a few weeks. It was therefore felt that bananas were a suitable export
crop for St Lucia if adequate shipping facilities could be obtained. The Commissioner
also notes, however, that between one hundred and three hundred labourers were
leaving for Panama to work on the Canal on every mailboat visiting the island.

298 **A general description of the island of St Lucia, 1787.**
M. Lefort de Latour. London: Colonial Office, 1787. Reprinted, 1883.
35p. (West India Papers, no. 44).

Written to accompany his map of the island (see item no. 24), the Royal Surveyor, M.
Lefort de Latour, provides in this description information on land ownership by whites
and free coloured people and indicates that 'family land' was already in existence. He
describes the extent of Crown Land and abandoned estates: of the 773 holdings
surveyed, 140 had reverted to the Crown because they were not being cultivated.
Crops grown on each holding are also listed and it is noted that, despite the hurricane
of 1780 which destroyed the town of Soufrière, the best bananas and cocoa were
grown in that part of the island. Lefort de Latour also points out that the lack of ports
on the windward side discouraged cultivation on that coast. Much land used for sugar
cultivation had been taken up for cotton production after the hurricane. This
publication was still in daily use in St Lucia as late as the mid-1960s as it was still the
only record of land ownership and property boundaries.

299 **Developing computerised monitoring and evaluation systems for
small agricultural development projects: lessons from the eastern
Caribbean.**
G. Mendelssohn. Brighton, England: Institute of Development
Studies, 1991. 50p. bibliog. (Discussion Paper, no. 294).

Addresses the practical difficulties that a development agency responsible for
implementing a number of small projects faces in establishing a capacity for

monitoring and ongoing evaluation with minimal resources. Lessons are drawn from work carried out to improve project implementation by establishing computerized information systems in Ministries of Agriculture in Dominica, Grenada and St Lucia.

300   **Caribbean transformations.**
Sidney W. Mintz.   Chicago: Aldine, 1974. 355p. bibliog.

Mintz looks at plantations and peasantries mainly in Puerto Rico, Haiti and Jamaica. St Lucia is considered in relation to its use of Creole and the survival of French folk customs and festivals.

301   **Agriculture in the West Indies: compiled from documents supplied to the West India Royal Commission, 1938-1939, and other sources.**
H. A. Tempany for the Colonial Office.   London: HMSO, 1942. 280p. maps.

Outlines the history of agricultural development, agricultural education and colonial agricultural administration in the Commonwealth West Indies.The chapter on St Lucia (p. 172-83) provides a general description of the island's environment, land ownership, food supplies, agriculture and forestry. Tempany notes that employment in the coaling industry and the presence of a garrison have attracted people to Castries and this has retarded the development of smallholding agriculture. Furthermore, indiscriminate forest clearance for cultivation on steep slopes has increased the problems of soil erosion, landslides and flooding. It is concluded that better farming methods among smallholders, the control of plant diseases and maintenance of soil fertility and a general diversification and increase in agricultural output is necessary to improve the standard of living for the island's inhabitants.

302   **Agricultural diversification: the experience of the Windward Islands.**
Mark Thomas.   Brighton, England: Institute of Development Studies, 1989. 32p. bibliog. map. (Discussion Paper, no. 257).

The preliminary research results on agricultural diversification in the four Windward Islands are presented here. Bananas have dominated the economies of the islands for three decades but efforts are now being made to move away from this monoculture. There are ten potential reasons which justify diversification, of which the most important are the dangers of dependency, risk and environmental hazards.

303   **Agricultural development in the Eastern Caribbean: a survey prepared by an AID survey team visiting Antigua, Barbados, Dominica, Grenada, Montserrat, St Kitts-Nevis (Anguilla), St Lucia, St Vincent.**
US Agency for International Development.   Washington, DC: US Agency for International Development, 1977. 335p.

Based on government documents and interviews with officials, this survey considers countries which have a large share of their Gross Domestic Product in agriculture (St Lucia has twenty-one per cent) but which experienced an agricultural productivity stagnation or decline in the 1970s resulting in dependence on food imports. For St

Lucia the report states that women constituted forty-three per cent of farm operators and unpaid family workers and thirty-five per cent of paid agricultural workers. It notes that eighty-two per cent of holdings are of less than five acres and about one-fifth of holdings have multiple owners. The Extension Service is described as one of the best in the region.

Report on vegetable production and the tourist industry in St Lucia.
See item no. 101.

Migration and rural development in the Caribbean.
See item no. 152.

Agricultural statistical digest 1984: St Lucia.
See item no. 390.

Final report on the 1986 census of agriculture of St Lucia.
See item no. 396.

Small-scale farming

304 **The social and cultural factors involved in production by small farmers in St Lucia of bananas and tomatoes and their marketing.**
Joyce Cole. Paris: UNESCO, 1981. 95p. bibliog.
The sample of twenty-two small-farm banana producers used for this study was drawn from the communities of Mon Repos, Saltibus and Grace/Belle Vue. The farmers had a modal age of more than sixty years old, none had more than a primary education and two-thirds of their holdings were less than five acres. Only two women farmers were included in the banana producers' sample, while out of the twenty tomato growers five were women. All the tomato growers were located in the Black Bay/Augier/Choiseul area in the south of the island. These farmers were younger than the banana growers and the youngest, two men in their early twenties, had some secondary education.

305 **Rural development in the Caribbean.**
Edited by P. I. Gomes. London: C. Hurst & Company; New York: St Martin's Press, 1985. 246p. maps.
This work consists of twelve chapters concerning rural development in the Caribbean. Three of the contributions provide a historical background while others illustrate the range of strategies adopted in the region since the mid-1950s. Two chapters deal specifically with St Lucia: chapter one, 'Peasant development in the West Indies since 1838' by Woodford K. Marshall situates the development of small farming in St Lucia in relation to the rest of the anglophone Caribbean; while a chapter by Yvonne Acosta and Jean Casimir on 'Social origins of the counter-plantation system in St Lucia' details its development since 1793 and the role of land tenure in influencing the growth of a new class structure.

306   **St Lucia.**
Elsa R. LeFranc.   In: *Small farming in the less developed countries of the Commonwealth Caribbean.*   Prepared by Weir's Agricultural Consulting Services.   Bridgetown: Caribbean Development Bank, 1980, p. 93-143.

In this description of small farming on St Lucia, the author shows that women are becoming increasingly important as the paid and unpaid labour force on small farms.

307   **Tubercules, bananes et legumes: le trio de productions d'une agriculture insulaire.** (Root crops, bananas and vegetables: the produce trio of an insular agriculture).
Paul Luu.   Castries: Ministry of Agriculture; Montpellier, France: Centre National d'Etudes Agronomiques des Régions Chaudes, 1985. 108p. maps. bibliog.

This is the report of a study carried out in 1984-85 of an area in south-west St Lucia near Choiseul. The study looks at systems of farming in the area and develops a typology based on the dominant crops (bananas, root crops, vegetables), on the proportion of cash and subsistence production, and on the ratio of perennial to annual cropping. Also covered is the production of what are termed marginal vegetables, in which category are included peanuts, pineapples and cannabis. There are six case-studies for which detailed information on returns for the various crops and on the agricultural calendar is provided.

308   **Small scale farming in Barbados, St Lucia and Martinique.**
J. D. Momsen.   In: *Proceedings of the Fifth West Indian Agricultural Economics Conference on the role of the small-scale farmer in the Caribbean economy.*   Edited by Dayanand Maharaj, John Strauss.
St Augustine, Trinidad: University of the West Indies, 1970, p. 78-84.

Comparisons are made based on detailed farm surveys in all three islands. Within each island farm production patterns are influenced by rainfall and by the proximity of markets. Each island had a characteristic basic food crop: eddoes in Barbados; tannia in St Lucia; and dasheen in Martinique. Most Barbadian small farmers employed labour while few in St Lucia and Martinique did so although St Lucia had the largest average farm size. More farmers in Barbados and Martinique also had off-farm jobs than in St Lucia, where, in addition, farms were less likely to have access to piped water, transportation and mechanical agricultural equipment than in the other two islands.

309   **Changing gender roles in Caribbean peasant agriculture.**
Janet Henshall Momsen.   In: *Small farming and peasant resources in the Caribbean.*   Edited by John S. Brierley, Hymie Rubenstein.
Winnipeg, Manitoba: University of Manitoba, Department of Geography, 1988, p. 83-100. (Manitoba Geographical Studies, no. 10).

The author looks at gender roles in small farming in several Eastern Caribbean islands. She finds that the proportion of women farmers in St Lucia has declined from forty-three per cent in 1964 to twenty-three per cent in 1980 and is even lower in commercially-oriented small farming.

310 **Small scale agriculture in St Lucia.**
G. R. J. Rapai. MA thesis, University of Western Ontario, London, Ontario, 1984. 245p. maps. bibliog.
A sample survey of eighty-three small farmers was carried out in 1979 and the results are reported in this study. The sample was stratified by eight soil categories and the results are compared to Momsen's 1965 survey. The average age of farmers is the same, at forty-seven years of age, but the proportion of women farmers had declined and there was greater farm fragmentation.

311 **Small farmers and their socio-economic impact: a case study from Tête Chemin, St Lucia.**
Wolf-Dietrich Sahr. Saarbrücken, Germany; Fort Lauderdale, Florida: Verlag Breitenback Publishers, 1987. 201p. maps. bibliog.
After reviewing the history of agricultural development in St Lucia, the author, on the basis of interviews with thirty-one of the 129 farmers in the inland village of Tête Chemin, describes the agro-ecotypes that predominate. He discusses the island's economic dependence on bananas and provides suggestions for improving cropping systems, infrastructure and marketing. In the conclusion he considers the possibilities of eco-development in an export-oriented smallholder society.

312 **A profile of small farmers in the Caribbean region.**
Clarence Zuvekas Jr. Washington, DC: US Department of Agriculture and Agency for International Development, Office of International Co-operation and Development, Sector Analysis Internalization Group, 1978. 101p. bibliog.
Data is presented on Barbados and the Windward and Leeward Islands plus the British Virgin Islands and the Turks and Caicos Islands in this profile. The information is based on the 1970 Population Census of the Commonwealth Caribbean, agricultural censuses taken between 1971 and 1975 and various sample surveys of small farmers. Topics covered include farm household characteristics, standard-of-living indicators, land tenure, production and the provision of government services to small farmers. Research showed that farmers in St Lucia were younger and less well educated than in the other islands. About twenty per cent of the island's small farms were held under family land tenure which limited access to credit but this problem was being overcome by the Caribbean Development Bank.

'An equal right to the soil': the rise of a peasantry in St Lucia 1838-1900.
See item no. 145.

Empirical testimony: the case of the Mabouya Valley in St Lucia.
See item no. 211.

Report on the Round Table on the participation and integration of women in agriculture and rural development in the Caribbean, Castries, 6-10 July, 1987.
See item no. 214.

Towards a recognition of the 'invisible' women in agriculture and rural development in St Lucia.
See item no. 215.

Woman-headed households, the sexual division of labour and agriculture: a case study in St Lucia, West Indies.
See item no. 222.

Reasons for the neglect of women in agriculture by agricultural extension officers, St Lucia.
See item no. 223.

Livestock

313   **Dermatophilosis of cattle, sheep and goats in St Lucia.**

M. C. Butler.   *State Veterinary Journal* (1975), p. 279-83.

Examines the outbreak of dermatophilosis (*Dermatophilus congolense*) in 1972-73, which was possibly the first report of the disease from the West Indies. Butler describes how it was confined to a relatively small area of the island where the tick *Amblyomma variegatum*, which appears to be the main means of spreading the disease, is also found. The disease is severe, causing extensive lesions in cattle, sheep and goats with mortality in all three species, although morbidity is lower in goats. It is suggested that tick control may lead to the elimination of the disease.

314   **Ticks on livestock in St Lucia.**

G. I. Garris, K. Scotland.   *Veterinary Parasitology*, vol. 18 (1985), p. 376-473.

Ticks and tick-borne diseases are a major obstacle to livestock production on St Lucia. The authors of this study examined cattle, sheep, goats and horses for tick infestation. They found that over ninety-five per cent of Holstein cross-breeds, twenty-eight per cent of sheep, and eighteen per cent of goats were infested with southern cattle tick, *Boophilus microplus Canestrini*. The livestock also suffered from tropical horse tick, *Anocentor nitens Neumann*, and tropical bont tick, *Amblyomma variegatum Fabricius*.

315   **Seroprevalence of Anaplasmosis and Babesiosis in livestock on St Lucia, 1983.**

M. E. Hugh-Jones, K. Scotland, L. M. Applewhaite, F. M. Alexander. *Tropical Animal Health Production*, vol. 20 (1988), p. 137-39.

Presents the results of a study involving 251 cattle from 31 different herds, and 54 sheep and 22 goats from 13 separate flocks. The animals were sampled for antibodies to *Anaplasma marginale*, *Babesia bigemina*, and *B. bovis*. The authors found that seventy-three per cent of the sampled cattle were seropositive for *A. marginale*, seventy per cent tested positive for *B. bigemina*, and fifty-six per cent for *B. bovis*. Lower seroprevalences (between twenty and forty per cent) were found in the sheep and goats.

316 **Clinical and serological evidence of bovine babesiosis and anaplasmosis in St Lucia.**
R. T. Knowles, M. Montrose, T. M. Craig, G. G .Wagner, R. F. Long.
Veterinary Parasitology, vol. 10, no. 4 (1982), p. 307-11. bibliog.
The authors compare results from indirect fluorescent antibody tests and Anaplasma card tests on imported calves and native cattle for bovine babesiosis and anaplasmosis.

317 **Distribution of heartwater in the Caribbean determined on the basis of detection of antibodies to the conserved 32-kilodalton protein of *Cowdria ruminantium*.**
Anneke Muller Kobold, Dominique Martinez, Emmanuel Camus, Frans Jongejan. *Journal of Clinical Microbiology,* vol. 30, no. 7 (1992), p. 1,870-73.
A total of 1,804 serum samples was collected from cattle on nineteen islands in the Eastern Caribbean and tested. Some 133 serum samples from ten islands, including St Lucia, were found to be positive This study shows that the causative agent of heartwater is now firmly established in St Lucia.

318 **The occurrence of streptothricosis and its association with *Amblyomma variegatum* ticks in St Lucia.**
A. N. Morrow, E. A. Compton. *Zentralblatt für Veterinarmedizin: Reihe B.*, vol. 38, no. 8 (Oct. 1991), p. 635-38.
Cattle, horses, goats and sheep in all areas of St Lucia were examined to ascertain the prevalence and distribution of streptothricosis on the island. Its association with the occurrence of *Amblyomma variegatum* ticks was also investigated. Although the disease was found to occur throughout St Lucia it was more prevalent and generally took a more severe form when *A. variegatum* ticks were present. A tick control programme in the north of the island appeared to have contributed to a dramatic reduction in the prevalence of streptothricosis disease.

319 **Economic development in the Eastern Caribbean Islands: St Lucia: series 1 livestock development.**
Barry Nestel. Barbados: University of the West Indies, Institute of Social and Economic Research (Eastern Caribbean), 1964. 130p.
This work reports on observations made by the author during a visit to the island. In the face of increasing imports of meat and dairy products it is suggested that there is considerable scope for an expansion of grassland farming. The Vieux Fort Peasant Grazing area has been very costly and has led to over-grazing and thus it is very important that it should become self-supporting and sustainable. There is also a need for careful breeding of cattle and pigs with imported stock. The introduction of sheep in the Vieux Fort area is proposed.

320 **Preweaning growth performance of Santa Gertrudis, Jamaica Red and Guernsey crossbred calves in St Lucia, West Indies.**
R. Rastogi, C. Hennecart, S. Tontinelle. *Tropical Agriculture,* vol. 56, no. 4 (Oct. 1979), p. 321-26. bibliog.
The early growth performance of Santa Gertrudis, Jamaica Red and Guernsey crossbred calves was analysed over a period of six years in order to study differences in the growth of the calves due to the type of breeding practised. It was concluded that differences related to breeding were significant for birth weight only with Santa Gertrudis calves having the highest average birth weight.

Sugar cane

321 **Report of the technical committee to consider government's proposals to Sugar Manufacturers Ltd on restructuring the sugar industry at Roseau.**
J. W. Daniel, R. D. E. Yearwood, Donald B. Louisey. Castries: Ministry of Trade and Industry, 1964. 9p.
The last sugar crop in St Lucia was in 1963 and by 1964 the fields were planted in bananas. The committee indicated that the earliest sugar harvest would therefore not be until 1966. Small farmers were keen to return to sugar cultivation but the large growers felt that there was little chance of resurrecting the industry. As this would require a subsidy from the government, the committee did not recommend restructuring the industry but suggested that land settlements could be established in the former sugar valleys.

322 **Commission of enquiry into the sugar industry of St Lucia.**
Government of St Lucia. Castries: Government Printery, 1960. 25p.
The terms of reference of the Commission of enquiry were to examine the economics of the sugar industry. The Commission recommended improvements in the handling and transport of sugar cane and higher payments to cane farmers on delivery. New proposals which had been made on tenancy and the centralization of the manufacturing of sugar were approved.

323 **Extracts from the report of the West Indian Sugar Commission for the year 1929-30.**
Lord Olivier, D. M. Semple. Bridgetown: Government Printing Office, 1930. 124p.
A Commission was appointed to investigate the sugar industry because in the West Indies the industry was currently operating at a deficit and this was having a devastating effect on the welfare of the islands. Prices had fallen because of world overproduction and the Commissioners stated that if Imperial rates of preference were not increased the sugar crop would cease to be planted by 1931 as St Lucia could expect an increasing deficit on the year's finance. In the island, where sugar provided forty-five per cent of the value of exports, it was said that twenty-five per cent of the

working population of St Lucia would suffer if the sugar industry collapsed. Yields per acre were lower in St Lucia than in any of the other islands visited.

324 **Enquiry into the feasibility of re-introducing the sugar industry in St Lucia.**
B. Persaud, O. de Barry, P. Haynes, F. R. Hore, E. Mathurin, E. R. Ward. Cave Hill, Barbados: University of the West Indies, Institute of Social and Economic Research (Eastern Caribbean), 1966. 88p.
The authors describe the background to the Enquiry and the potential sugar cane growing area. They consider the re-establishment of the industry in the traditional sugar valleys, the costs .and returns of cane cultivation in the southern part of the island and the possibilities of manufacturing other products from cane.

Statement on the strike situation in the sugar valleys.
See item no. 389.

Other crops

325 **Screening for root-knot nematode (*Meloidogyne incognita* (Kofoid and White) Chitwood) resistance in certain lines of *Lycopersicon esculentum* Mill. for tomato improvement in St Lucia.**
S. R. Gowen, W. B. Charles. *Proceedings of the Tropical Region American Society of Horticultural Science*, vol. 12 (1968), p. 21-27. bibliog.
Reports on a simple method used to screen for resistance to root-node nematode in certain hybrid tomatoes derived from crossing promising high-yielding varieties with Nemared, a resistant variety. The hybrid plants had significantly fewer galls than susceptible varieties.

326 **Nutrition of coconuts in St Lucia and relationship with attack by coconut mite *Aceria geurreronis* Keifer.**
D. Moore, M. S. Ridout, L. Alexander. *Tropical Agriculture*, vol. 68, no. 1 (Jan. 1991), p. 41-44.
A leaf analysis of coconuts in St Lucia showed that only 2.5 per cent of trees had adequate levels of all three major nutrients, N, P and K. There was some association between nutrient status and levels of damage by the coconut mite, *Eriophyes guerreronis*. Damage was generally greater with increasing levels of nitrogen.

327 **Summary of results of tapping rubber trees at Dominica and St Lucia.**
J. C. Moore. *West Indian Bulletin: The Journal of the Imperial Agricultural Department for the West Indies,* vol. 8, no. 2 (1907), p. 204-08.

In the late 1890s *Castilloa elastica* rubber trees were planted as shade trees in cacao plantations in St Lucia. About 200 of these trees were between eight and twelve years old when this article was written and experiments with tapping for latex were carried out in 1905 on trees in the Botanic Garden. The author concludes that the results show that there can be no doubt as to the suitability of the greater part of St Lucia for the successful cultivation of the rubber tree.

328 **Performance of some heat tolerant tomatoes in St Lucia, East Caribbean.**
A. Sajjapongse. In: *Improved vegetable production in Asia.* Taipei: Food and Fertilization Center for the Asian and Pacific Region, 1987, p. 121-22.

Three field experiments were carried out on thirty-five varieties of tomato. Based on measurements of yield and yield attributes it was felt that the Caraibe variety was too heat sensitive. Three heat-tolerant varieties were found to be most suitable for growing in the hot season.

Fishing

329 **Last of the Caribbean whalemen.**
John E. Adams. *Natural History*, vol. 103, no. 11 (Nov. 1994), p. 64-72. map.

Describes the last four shore-based whaling operations still in existence in the region. Two operate out of St Vincent while the other two are based in Castries and Vieux Fort, with crews largely made up of elderly men. Whaling began in the Caribbean in the nineteenth century and at its peak (1880-1920) supported more than twenty whaling establishments in the south-eastern Caribbean. The International Whaling Commission (IWC) bans do not yet protect the small cetaceans, such as porpoises, dolphins and pilot whales, which are still hunted in the Windwards.

330 **A comparative study of the fisheries of Martinique and St Lucia.**
R. G. Cecil. MA thesis, McGill University, Montreal, 1966. maps. bibliog.

Cecil discusses the marine resources, the types of fishing boats and nets used, the production, marketing and viability of the fishing industry and the development plans proposed for these two islands. In St Lucia fishermen still use dugout canoes made from the white gum tree (*Dacryodes hexandra*) while these are dying out in Martinique. The author estimates that in 1966 St Lucia had 1,410 traditional fishermen producing eighty per cent of St Lucia's total catch of about 850,000 lbs per year or 10 lbs per person per year. He concludes that traditional fishing is not profitable and most fishermen are also small farmers.

331 **St Lucia dug-outs.**
Philip P. Chase. *American Neptune,* vol. 2, no. 1 (1942), p. 71-73.
Chase describes the construction and rough dimensions of the dug-outs as well as the sailing techniques of St Lucian fishermen.

Fisheries Training School in St Lucia.
See item no. 454.

West Indian sea magic.
See item no. 481.

To windward of the land: the occult world of Alexander Charles.
See item no. 482.

Banana Industry

Socio-economic aspects

332 Issues in the Windward-Jamaica banana war.
George Beckford. In: *Readings in the political economy of the Caribbean.* Edited by Norman Girvan, Owen Jefferson. Kingston: New World Group, 1971, p. 77-86. bibliog.

Jamaica was the main Commonwealth Caribbean producer of bananas from the nineteenth century right up until 1964, when the Windward Islands exported more to the British market than Jamaica. The competition between the two led to a fall in prices and the resulting conflict took place between two private marketing firms rather than between the growers. Bananas made up seventy per cent of the Windward Island's exports and eighty-five per cent of St Lucia's, while in Jamaica they accounted for only seven per cent of total exports.

333 Winban News: commemorative issue.
Edited by Aubrey V. Grell, John H. Pilgrim. Castries: The Voice Publishing Company, 1966. 26p. map.

This special illustrated issue of the *Winban News* commemorates the visit of the Queen and Prince Phillip to St Lucia and the opening of the WINBAN Research Laboratory and experimental station at Roseau by Her Majesty. It includes a history of the Windward Island Banana Growers' Association (WINBAN), banana production figures for 1958 to 1965, banana recipes and notes on uses of the banana.

334 St Lucia's banana industry.
A. L. Lam. *The Caribbean*, vol. 13, no. 8 (Aug. 1959), p. 154-55.

Describes the early years of the modern St Lucian banana industry following the contract signed with Geest Industries Ltd., which ensured the industry of a guaranteed market for the fruit. Production figures are given for the years 1954 to 1959. The number of stems exported from the island increased fourfold between 1954 and 1958 and the author estimates that 5,500 acres were planted in bananas. The St Lucia Banana Growers Association was formed in 1953 and by 1959 had a membership of 5,200 planters. The Association oversees the production and marketing of bananas and collects a cess from its members to help finance the control of pests and diseases. Plans were being made to develop a comprehensive programme of spraying to control banana leaf spot disease.

335 **Une période cruciale dans l'évolution de la bananerie antillaise: les années 1960-1980.** (A crucial period in the evolution of the West Indian banana industry: 1960-1980.)
Jean-Claude Maillard. *Revista Geográfica*, vol. 99 (1984), p. 109-20. bibliog.

Maillard compares the growth of the banana industry in the French West Indies and the Windward Islands. He states that, despite hurricanes which have affected both groups of islands, the relative prosperity of the French territories compared to the depression in the Windwards is caused by differences in their traditional markets.

336 **A banana costing study in St Lucia: the first report.**
B. Persaud. Barbados: University of the West Indies, Institute of Social and Economic Research (Eastern Caribbean), 1965. 46p. (Agricultural Series, no. 2).

Reports on a sample survey of the finances of banana farms in 1964. Eighty-eight farms were sampled, stratified by size and by location. Considerable variations in profit were found although the larger farms had lower returns per acre but higher returns in total.

337 **The second banana costing survey of St Lucia.**
Bishnodat Persaud. Cave Hill, Barbados: University of the West Indies, Institute of Social and Economic Research, 1967. 39p.

A survey of thirty farms in the main banana growing areas of the northern part of the island was undertaken in 1965, in which farms were stratified by size. The larger farms which covered more than ten acres had better land, were better managed and used fertilizer and labour more intensively than the smaller farms. Average profits per acre on small farms were only fifty-five per cent of those on the larger farms and yields of bananas were 286 stems per acre on small farms (average size 3.3 acres) compared with 427 stems per acre on the larger farms.

338 **The rural entrepreneur and economic development: the case of St Lucia.**
Rochelle S. Romalis. In: *McGill Studies in Anthropology*. Edited by Francis Henry. Montreal: McGill University Centre for Developing-Area Studies, 1969, p. 93-109. bibliog.

Describes the transformation of a peasant-proletariat, dependent on subsistence agriculture and plantation labour, into independent banana farmers owning fifty-seven per cent of the land, following the introduction of the banana industry in 1953. The analysis is based on a study of La Croix in the hilly interior of the island which was one of the poorest communities in St Lucia producing only cassava flour and charcoal.

Located only eight miles from Castries and benefitting from fertile land, the advent of bananas almost immediately brought considerable wealth to the area. Five individuals, distinguished by having worked abroad or on one of the American bases on the island as skilled or semi-skilled craftsmen, gave leadership and became community leaders.

339 **Economic change and peasant political consciousness in the Commonwealth Caribbean.**
Rochelle Romalis. *The Journal of Commonwealth and Comparative Politics*, vol. 8, no. 3 (Nov. 1975), p. 225-41. bibliog.

Romalis studies the shift to cash cropping, which occurred mainly in the 1950s, and the interaction of the peasant population with local political leaders in St Lucia. The Banana Growers Association made peasant producers aware of metropolitan manipulation as well as internal exploitation by their own political leadership. This led to political polarization and a struggle for power among various island factions during the 1960s. Reorganization of the Association resulted in the loss of control by both small growers and the middle-class board of directors under pressure from metropolitan interests. This incident is seen as making the rural population more politically conscious.

340 **Whose gold? Geest and the banana trade.**
Anne Simpson. London: Latin America Bureau, 1988. 33p. maps.

A study of the Windward Island banana trade and the role of the shipping and marketing company, Geest, through the eyes of people in Britain and the Caribbean. The book is written for use in schools by children aged between fourteen and sixteen years old.

341 **Assistance vital for banana industry survival.**
Jack Spector. *West Indies Chronicle*, vol. 86, no. 1,486 (Nov. 1971), p. 490.

In 1970, in an effort to improve fruit quality the banana growers of the Windward Islands initiated the system of boxing fruit, at considerable cost. However, drought in 1970 and in 1971 and heavy rainstorms reduced St Lucia's output of bananas by half. Since bananas accounted for ninety per cent of the visible exports of St Lucia, the island requested emergency assistance for a banana rehabilitation programme.

342 **Economic aspects of the banana industry in St Lucia.**
A. B. Tench. Castries: WINBAN, 1973. 118p.

This is one of the most thorough reports on the banana industry written at a time of declining production. This decline was linked to drought, alternative employment opportunities in the construction industry and a big increase in the price of fertilizer. Between 1966 and 1972 the price of bananas to the growers fell by twenty-five per cent, at a time when costs were increasing. Tench suggests that the industry should be revitalized and the contract with the shipping company amended.

343 **Cash crops and development: bananas in the Windward Islands.**
Mark Thomas. Brighton: Institute of Development Studies, 1989.
36p. bibliog. map. (Discussion Paper, no. 258).

Thomas presents an assessment of the position of bananas in the Windward Islands in the context of the wider cash crop debate. He discusses crop characteristics, the mode of production, government policies, employment, the environment and dependence and concludes that bananas could fuel growth but that the institutional framework of the industry and the characteristics of the crop have inhibited direct forward and backward linkages.

344 **Green gold: bananas and dependency in the Eastern Caribbean.**
Robert Thomson. London: Latin America Bureau, 1987. 93p. map.
bibliog.

In addition to a history of the banana industry in the Windward Islands, Thomson provides a description of the production and marketing processes and an analysis of the role of Geest plc in shipping and marketing. In the St Lucia case-study it is pointed out that the island was the first to export bananas and shipped forty-five per cent of the Windward's total exports in 1983. Geest owned 40,000 acres of prime farmland there until 1983. Over three-quarters of St Lucia's banana farmers work less than ten acres of farmland. They have limited access to credit and their yields are about half those of the large plantations. Thomson also notes that the industry received EC$4.3 million in aid between 1969 and 1979 and independence and hurricane damage led to the restructuring of the industry at the beginning of the 1980s.

345 **St Lucia's banana industry.**
E. A. Walters. *Tropical Agriculture*, vol. 5, no. 10 (Oct. 1928),
p. 247-49. bibliog.

An historical account of the inception and development of commercial banana planting in St Lucia, beginning with the proposal in 1922 by British interests of the development of large-scale banana cultivation in the island. In 1923 the Swift Banana Company planted fifteen acres of Gros Michel bananas but Panama disease, first noted in 1924, forced the abandonment of the original planting. Regular shipments to New York began in 1926 but these ended shortly afterwards when the promoting company went bankrupt. The total crop at that time was 10,500 to 12,500 bunches per month.

346 **Institutional structures as a factor in land-use decisions: the impact of Banana Growers Associations in French and Commonwealth islands in the Eastern Caribbean.**
Barbara M. Welch. PhD dissertation, University of London, 1989.
maps. bibliog.

Welch discusses the changing role of WINBAN and the individual island banana growers associations on agricultural land use in Guadeloupe, Martinique, Dominica, St Vincent, Grenada and St Lucia. The period covered is 1960 to 1980.

347 **Banana dependency: albatross or liferaft for the Windwards?**
Barbara Welch. *Social and Economic Studies,* vol. 43, no. 1 (1994),
p. 123-49. bibliog.
Examines the contention that the dependency on exporting bananas to European
countries, which is strongest in St Lucia, is inherently bad for the Windward Islands.
The author reviews the origins of the trade and evaluates the physical, economic and
social impact of banana exporting on St Lucia and Dominica. The average small
banana farmer on St Lucia produces only five tons per year but there appear to be no
real alternatives to bananas.

348 **Challenging economic irrelevance: the role of banana growers'**
associations in St Lucia and Martinique.
Barbara Welch. *Caribbean Geography*, vol. 4, no. 2 (1994),
p. 102-15. bibliog.
A discussion of the background to the development of banana cultivation in the
Eastern Caribbean and the rationale for producer associations in general provides the
context for an evaluation of the role played by banana growers' associations in St
Lucia and Martinique. The relationship between the socio-economic profile of their
members and the policies pursued is examined and the impact of the interventions of
the associations on the location of cultivation and level of output is considered.
Numbers of banana growers in St Lucia fell from 12,000 in 1966 to under 7,000 in
1986 but the association remained more broadly based than that in Martinique.

349 **The impact of 'Hurricane Allen' on the St Lucia banana industry.**
Mervin C. Williams. *Caribbean Geography*, vol. 2, no. 3 (Oct. 1988),
p. 164-72. bibliog.
On 3-4 August 1980 St Lucia was devastated by Hurricane Allen. The hurricane
destroyed all the standing banana crop, killed six people and made 9,600 homeless.
The total estimated damage and income losses were put at EC$235, 410,000, of which
seventy-nine per cent was in agriculture. A banana rehabilitation programme which
included fiscal incentives for farmers, subsidized inputs for banana growing,
improvements in feeder roads and field packing of the fruit, was undertaken.
Seventeen months after the storm, the value of banana exports was eight per cent
higher than before the hurrricane.

The social and cultural factors involved in production by small farmers
in St Lucia of bananas and tomatoes and their marketing.
See item no. 304.

Tubercules, bananes et legumes: le trio de productions d'une agriculture
insulaire. (Root crops, bananas and vegetables: the produce trio of an insular
agriculture.)
See item no. 307.

An abstract of West Indian banana statistics (with special reference to
the Windward Islands).
See item no. 404.

Agronomic aspects

350 **Factors affecting the severity of deflowering latex stain on banana bunches in the Windward Islands.**
Nigel H. Banks. *Tropical Agriculture*, vol. 67, no. 2 (1990), p. 111-14.
The removal of flower parts from the banana plant results in a latex release that stains the fruit and commercial banana producers are constantly seeking methods of reducing latex stain. This research demonstrates that the greatest control of latex stain could be obtained by restricting deflowering operations to the middle of the day.

351 **Nematicidal effects of foliar applications of oxamyl to banana seedlings.**
S. R. Gowen. *Nematropica*, vol. 5, no. 2 (1975), p. 22. bibliog.
Gowen reports how foliar applications of oxamyl prevented nematodes from invading banana roots. In this way nematode invasion may be prevented for up to eight weeks after treatment. Oxamyl applied to nematode-infested plants gave incomplete control.

352 **Varietal responses and prospects for breeding nematode resistant banana varieties.**
S. R. Gowen. *Nematropica*, vol. 6, no. 2 (1976), p. 45-49.
Diploid, triploid and tetraploid banana clones were evaluated for their response to attack by *Radopholus similis* and *Helicotylenchus multicinctus*. It was found that the cultivated diploid clone 'Sukuzani' was marginally less susceptible to these nematodes than two other diploids. Gowen therefore concluded that the first requirement in developing a programme for nematode resistance will be to locate a suitable source of resistance in wild varieties.

353 **Nematicidal effects of oxamyl applied to leaves of banana seedlings.**
S. R. Gowen. *Journal of Nematology*, vol. 9, no. 2 (1977), p. 158-61.
Work carried out at the WINBAN research station showed that the spraying of leaves of banana seedlings significantly reduced nematode invasion.

354 **Effects of irrigation at critical stages of ontogeny of the banana cultivar robusta on growth and yield.**
Gordon D. Holder, Frank A. Gumbs. *Tropical Agriculture*, vol. 59, no. 3 (July 1982), p. 221-26.
Field trials showed that irrigation in the third sixty-day period after planting significantly increased pseudostem height and girth and reduced the time between planting and bunch emergence.

355 **Agronomic assessment of the relative suitability of the banana cultivars Robusta and Giant Cavendish (Williams hybrid) to irrigation.**
Gordon D. Holder, Frank A. Gumbs. *Tropical Agriculture*, vol. 60, no. 1 (Jan. 1983), p. 17-24.
Failure to establish significant and economically important differences between the two cultivars, 'Robusta' and 'Giant Cavendish', in fruit yield per plant strongly supports 'Giant Cavendish' as a more efficient fruit producer than 'Robusta' since the former is significantly shorter and therefore less liable to wind damage. 'Giant Cavendish' outyields 'Robusta' by 13.4 per cent over three cropping cycles in St Lucia.

356 **Effects of irrigation on the growth and yield of banana.**
Gordon D. Holder, Frank A. Gumbs. *Tropical Agriculture*, vol. 60, no. 1 (Jan. 1983), p. 25-30. bibliog.
'Robusta' bananas were grown as a plant crop under four irrigation regimes in St Lucia. No significant growth response was detected but significant increases in fruit yield were obtained from treatments irrigated to sixty-six per cent and seventy-five per cent of soil available moisture.

357 **Effects of waterlogging on the growth and yield of bananas.**
Gordon D. Holder, Frank A. Gumbs. *Tropical Agriculture*, vol. 60, no. 2 (April 1983), p. 111-16, 57.
Bananas growing on land prone to waterlogging in St Lucia gave a reduced harvested fruit yield. The times to bunch emergence and harvesting were also delayed. It was discovered that over irrigation led to reductions in the number of fingers per hand and hands per bunch, yet the bunches were heavier than the non-irrigated control because of an increase in finger length.

358 **Leaf characteristics for the identification of the banana cultivars 'Robusta' and 'Giant Cavendish'.**
G. D. Holder, G. Taylor. *Tropical Agriculture*, vol. 63, no. 2 (April 1986), p. 117-20, 162.
Leaf characteristics, leaf index and leaf area were used to identify the banana cultivars 'Robusta' and 'Giant Cavendish'. Two discriminant functions are presented and discussed.

359 **Supplemental irrigation of bananas in St Lucia.**
A. Madramootoo, P. J. Jutras. *Agricultural Water Management*, vol. 9 (1984), p. 149-56.
It is suggested in this article that the decline in output of bananas after 1970 may be partly due to lower total annual rainfall. An experimental irrigation project was designed and soil and crop characteristics measured over a two-year period. Yield increases of 7.3 per cent in the plant crop and 4.3 per cent in the second ratoon crop were noted. Irrigation was found to reduce the number of days to harvest and to increase leaf production, whilst the heavy montmorillonitic clay soils caused some problems in the application of water.

360 **Report on a banana acreage survey of the Windward Islands.**
Janet D. Momsen. London: Overseas Development Ministry, 1969.
50p. map. bibliog.

This survey of the banana lands of the four Windward Islands was carried out in 1965 and 1966. Land in bananas is classified on the basis of pure stands and mixed stands. In the case of St Lucia the 1:50,000 map of banana lands shows five classes: bananas in pure stands; bananas and coconuts; bananas and tree crops; bananas and mixed crops; and bananas and forest. In 1965 St Lucia had 33,666 acres of bananas of which fifty-five per cent was in the low density bananas and mixed crop class and only 14.5 per cent in pure stands. There were 12,478 registered growers of whom ninety-eight per cent were small farmers. These farmers contributed forty-eight per cent of the export bananas from sixty-one per cent of the total banana acreage. The yield per acre for small farmers was only 148 stems while estates averaged 252 stems per acre.

361 **Field trials with three molluscides in banana cultivation.**
R. F. Sturrock, G. Barnish, J. Seeyave. *Pflanzenschutznachr Bayer*,
vol. 27, no. 1 (1974), p. 57-62.

The authors report on tests with applications of three molluscides to young banana trees, which showed no phytotoxic effects nor left any residue on the bananas. It was concluded that these could be used as a control measure against the aquatic snails which play a role in the transmission of schistosomiasis.

362 **Banana investigations 1962.**
I. T. Twyford in consultation with R. F. Barnes, L. Kasasian, P. Moss,
L. H. Smith, D. Walmsley. Trinidad: University of the West Indies,
Imperial College of Tropical Agriculture, Soil and Land Use Section of
the Regional Research Centre, 1962. 37p. (Section Report, no. 7).

Discusses eight fertilizer trials on bananas in St Lucia and suggests that the optimum fertilizer for the NPK deficient soils typical of St Lucia should be in the ratio 12:12:30. It notes the effect of nitrogen in reducing the time to crop in bananas.

363 **Fungi associated with crown-rot disease of bananas from St Lucia
in the Windward Islands.**
Ann Wallbridge, J. A. Pinegar. *Transactions of the British Mycology
Society*, vol. 64, no. 2 (1975), p. 247-54.

The authors consider the problem of crown-rot disease, which has been a serious factor limiting the commercialization of bananas in the Windward Islands. It is associated with the practice of packing the fruit in fibreboard boxes as complete hands rather than shipping them on the stem. Decay of the crown tissue makes the fruit unattractive and more difficult to handle. Treatment used in Australia and the Cameroons was tested and the fungi shown to be insensitive to this treatment identified.

**Notes on a botanical and soil inspection of the St Lucia banana and
forest lands.**
See item no. 41.

Land Tenure and Settlement

Land tenure

364 **Land tenure and development in the Eastern Caribbean.**
Edited by Frank W. Alleyne. Bridgetown, Barbados: Carib Research
and Publications, 1994. 170p. map.

These are the proceedings of a symposium held a decade earlier in St Lucia, which
focused on Beckford's thesis that rural development in the Caribbean was constrained
by plantation resource allocation. The late Professor George Beckford's keynote
address is included along with seven papers, discussion sessions and three workshop
reports. Frank Alleyne's paper on land tenure, credit and agricultural development in
the lesser developed countries of CARICOM concludes that St Lucia has 'the most
complex pattern of tenure among the LDCs in CARICOM'. He suggests that family
land has declined to less than ten per cent of arable land but that the lack of title and
security of tenure are major problems restricting the availability of credit facilities to
small farmers. A table based on data from a 1979 WINBAN survey shows nine
subsets of rental tenure with only about half the renters having the security of a
contractual arrangement.

365 **A comparative evaluation framework for cadastre-based land
information systems (CLIS) in developing countries.**
Grenville Barnes. PhD thesis, University of Wisconsin, Madison,
1988. bibliog. (Available from University Microfilms International,
Ann Arbor, Michigan, order no. DA 8820035).

Problems of rural poverty are being countered by the strengthening of private land
rights and the improvement of public institutions through the implementation of CLIS.
The comparative evaluation framework developed in this study makes use of the CLIS
model to describe the systems in Honduras, Ecuador and St Lucia. These systems are
evaluated on the basis of six criteria.

366 **Family land and development in St Lucia.**
Christine Barrow. Cave Hill, Barbados: University of the West
Indies, Institute of Social and Economic Research (Eastern Caribbean),
1992. 83p. maps. (Monograph Series, no. 1).

This study provides an alternative view to the traditional condemnation of the family
land system as anachronistic, wasteful and a barrier to agricultural modernization. In
contrast to this, Barrow interprets the internal logic and functioning of family land, in
both historical and contemporary periods, within its own ideological perspective and
socio-economic and cultural context. She includes a case-study of the village of Tête
Chemin, which is located in the centre of the island on steep, hilly land and was only
established some sixty years ago by migrants from the crowded coastal areas.
Information on the family land in the village did not support many of the criticisms of
this system found in literature on the subject. The monograph concludes that
government policies aimed at rationalizing land tenure and commoditizing agricultural
land strike at the very essence of family land and threaten to reverse the historical
process of land redistribution, independent peasant cultivation and social equity in St
Lucia.

367 **Family land tenure and agricultural development in St Lucia.**
John W. Bruce. Madison, Wisconsin: University of Wisconsin Press,
1978. 59p. (Land Tenure Center Research Paper, no. 78).

Provides a review of the literature on family land tenure in St Lucia and proposes a
research programme to begin before the planned cadastral survey and land
registration. The family land system has reduced the incidence of land fragmentation
but makes it difficult to obtain credit and such land is not easily marketable.

368 **Historical account of land tenure systems in the Caribbean.**
Caribbean Economic Review, vol. 1, nos. 1-2 (Dec. 1949), p. 133-52.

This article discusses the system of free grants of land which were made to French
subjects after St Lucia was ceded to France in 1763. This land had to be cultivated to a
satisfactory standard within a certain period of time or it reverted to the Crown. Such
reverted lands became known as 'Abandonné et Réunie Au Domain du Roi' (ABR
lands). Before 1903 these lands were advertised to ascertain if any owners or
claimants existed and if there were none then the land was vested in the Crown. After
1903, however, all lands, whether ABR or ungranted, had to be surveyed and
claimants sought. Only if no claims were filed was the land then vested in the Crown.
Provision was also made in the case of grantees who had been absent from the colony
for more than 100 years and had abandoned their grants of land, for the Crown to
survey and escheat these lands.

369 **Land tenure in the Caribbean.**
Caribbean Economic Review, vol. 2, no. 2 (Nov. 1950), p. 124.

St Lucian land leases are governed by the St Lucia Civil Code and are usually under
the metayage or share cropping system where the landlord receives one-third of the
crop. Agricultural work is paid on the basis of tasks carried out, with different
minimum wages set for men, for women and for children. The article examines the
1938 land settlement scheme for 200 Barbadian families near Vieux-Fort which was
dislocated by the establishment of the United States Base; in 1948 these lands were
developed for another settlement scheme to employ some 1,000 St Lucian workers

growing rice and possibly sea island cotton. Loans to peasant farmers, for one to five years, were available as from 1940 on the condition that the holding was between three and fifty acres, that measures were taken to prevent soil erosion and that loans for fertilizer were approved by the Department of Agriculture.

370 **Coutume de Paris to 1988: the evolution of land law in St Lucia.**
Winston F. Cenec. Castries: Voice Press, [n.d.]. 131p.

This book reviews land law prior to the reforms of 1984. It also reviews the Land Acts of 1984-87 and offers a summary of the new reforms. The retrospective chapters include a review of the sources of Civil Law with a focus on the Civil Code of 1879 and a summary of the deed registration system up to 1984. The chapters dealing with the recent legislation review the aims of the Land Acts and summarize the new system of registration of titles. The author concludes that the effects of the most recent reforms are yet to be seen as the legislation is still in a transitional period.

371 **Socio-political aspects of land tenure in St Lucia.**
Joyce Cole. In: *Land tenure and development in the Eastern Caribbean.* Edited by Frank W. Alleyne. Bridgetown, Barbados: Carib Research and Publications, 1994, p. 79-103. bibliog.

Cole concentrates on a study of multiple land ownership, sharecropping and squatting. She finds that probably one-third of small farmers have some family land and that overall, the system of land tenure has led to severe land fragmentation, cultivation of steep hillsides with consequent land and forest degradation, general rural poverty and weak community organization. In addition, migration from rural areas both to Castries and overseas has resulted in labour shortages. Family land tenure reduces fragmentation and plays an important role in providing the symbolic security of land ownership.

372 **Patterns of land tenure in the Leeward and Windward Islands.**
H. J. Finkel. In: *Peoples and cultures of the Caribbean.* Edited by M. Horowitz. New York: Natural History Press, 1971, p. 291-304. bibliog.

Focuses on the issue of family land in St Lucia as a peculiar characteristic of the island, viewing it as a problem hindering agricultural development.

373 **Farm fragmentation in the Commonwealth Caribbean.**
T. L. Hills, S. Iton, J. Lundgren. In: *Proceedings of the Seventh West Indies Agricultural Economics Conference.* St Augustine, Trinidad: University of the West Indies, 1972, p. 88-102. bibliog.

In this paper the authors take a look at farm fragmentation in relation to farm management, land use and marketing. They suggest that community property or family land, as seen in St Lucia and Dominica, is only slightly used because of the negative effects of rights of usufruct.

374   **Rural land tenure systems in St Lucia.**
Elsa R.-M. LeFranc.   Mona, Jamaica: University of the West Indies,
Institute of Social and Economic Research, 1993. 92p. bibliog.
(Working Paper, no. 40).

This study draws on data collected during four months fieldwork in a St Lucian village
in 1975. It was submitted for publication in 1982 but languished for a decade in the
vaults of the publications section of the Institute of Social and Economic Research.
Yet, despite the delay the findings are still relevant. LeFranc notes the flexibility of the
family land system in terms of inheritance and return migrants as well as the
importance of kinship in determining access to land and residence in the community,
and the decline of exchange labour. The conclusion that the growth of the banana
industry with its accompanying individualization of land and land hunger, has led to
many of the problems which are often assumed to be due to family land tenure was
quite radical at the time of her study but is now widely accepted.

375   **Land tenure in St Lucia.**
D. C. E. Mathurin.   In: *Proceedings of the Second West Indian
Agricultural Economics Conference.*   St Augustine, Trinidad:
University of the West Indies, 1967, p. 139-52.

Reviews the family land system in St Lucia. This tenure system is seen as imposing
serious restrictions on the development of a rational land use policy.

376   **Land tenure as a barrier to agricultural innovation: the case of
St Lucia.**
J. D. Momsen.   In: *Proceedings of the Seventh West Indian
Agricultural Economics Conference.*   Edited by Osborne Nurse.
Trinidad: University of the West Indies, 1972, p. 103-09. map.

Considers the relationship between land tenure and the adoption of commercial
vegetable farming in St Lucia, based on a 1971 survey of sixty-eight farms
constituting a thirty-five per cent sample of all vegetable farms. It was found that the
mean size was 7.5 acres which is larger than the average size for small farms of 2.5
acres reported by the 1961 Agricultural Census. Multivariate analysis of the data
revealed that only a very small proportion of the total interfarm variation was
accounted for by land tenure.

377   **St Lucia natural resources and agriculture development project.**
OAS, Department of Regional Development.   Washington, DC:
Economic and Social Affairs, OAS, 1986. 253p. maps. bibliog.

Suggests studies and proposals for the implementation of a land registration
programme and describes rural settlements, land tenure, resources, conservation and
environmental planning.

378 **Reform among the smallholders: St Lucia, Jamaica and the implications for the Caribbean.**
Randy Stringer, John Bruce, David Stanfield. In: *Searching for agrarian reform in Latin America.* Edited by William C. Thiesenhusen. Boston, New York; London: Unwin Hyman, 1989, p. 338-57. bibliog.

The St Lucian titling programme is described in this paper. This was undertaken in order to reduce the insecurity of tenure and to increase productivity through access to credit and investment. It is stressed that careful monitoring of the titling initiative is needed and that a continuing evaluation of its impact on agricultural output, labour, distribution patterns, credit access, income and the balance between food and export crops must be undertaken.

379 **Common property in the Eastern Caribbean: family land tenure in economy and society in St Lucia, West Indies.**
John Carter Thornburg. PhD thesis, University of Wisconsin, Madison, 1990. bibliog. (Available from University Microfilms International, Ann Arbor, Michigan, order no. DA 9030813).

The objectives of this research were to understand the rules and structures of family land and to compare the impact of this form of tenure with that of farmers operating on privately owned land. There are agreed upon rules governing property and harvesting rights and conflict usually arises over boundaries or rights of trespass rather than harvest. Family land was found not to promote insecurity of tenure. Family land operators use significantly fewer inputs and have fewer cash crop trees than farmers on individually owned land but there was no difference in levels of investment in drainage schemes.

Land settlement

380 **Land Settlement Scheme for Saint Lucia based on a survey of the agricultural and social conditions of the island.**
R. A. Foreman. Castries: Government Printer, 1958. 15p.

Foreman suggests that land settlements could both eliminate much of the soil erosion caused by peasant shifting cultivation on steep slopes and also, by reducing population pressure on family lands, make it possible to reform the land tenure system. His recommendations were not acted upon.

381 **Land settlement as an imposed solution.**
Janet Henshall Momsen. In: *Land and development in the Caribbean.* Edited by Jean Besson, Janet Momsen. London; Basingstoke, England: Macmillan, 1988, p. 68-96. map. bibliog.

Discusses the role of land settlement in the development of small-scale agriculture in the Eastern Caribbean. Examples are drawn from Nevis, Montserrat, St Vincent and St

Lucia, with the two case-studies in St Lucia being the Vieux Fort settlement and the St Lucia Farms project.

382   **Roseau Valley Smallholders Crop Diversification Project St Lucia.**
      St Lucia Model Farms Ltd.   Castries: St Lucia Model Farms Ltd.,
      31 Jan. 1985. 6p.

The project was conceived by the landowners Geest Industries (Estates) Ltd. in 1976, and by 1985 fifty-nine farmers had been settled on the land. The delay in implementation was largely due to difficulties in finding a form of land tenure which would avoid land fragmentation. Farmers are offered leasehold holdings with an option to purchase for $100 after fifteen years. The project provides for the development of 1,600 acres of the Roseau Estate into model agricultural holdings for 184 participants. Valley holdings of five acres each are based on banana cultivation while terraced hillside holdings of ten to fifteen acres are expected to grow fruit and tree crops. The first phase of the project cost US $6.6 million.

383   **Peasant holding scheme in St Lucia.**
      Jay R. Singh.   *New Commonwealth*, vol. 21, no. 9 (June 1951),
      p. 688-90.

The Vieux Fort Land Utilisation Scheme, set up in 1949, was aimed at returning those workers who had been dependent on wage labour at the United States Army and Air Base to agricultural activities. It was planned to allocate plots of up to ten acres from the 1,400 acres of cultivable government land in the area. Singh reports that 488 peasant families occupied 900 acres and produced mainly rice and potatoes. The Central Farm provided four days work every two weeks for 1,000 workers.

Planning for women in rural development: a source book for the Caribbean.
See item no. 224.

Transport

384 Preliminary report of air and ocean transportation in selected countries of the Caribbean.
Jose Ysern de la Cruz.   Puerto Rico: Caribbean Organization, 1963. 81p.

This is the first report by the transportation sub-committee of the Caribbean Organization which was set up to review the transport problems of the countries of the region and to recommend measures by which these difficulties could be overcome. Questionnaires were sent out to all the countries served by the Caribbean Organization but only twelve, including St Lucia, responded. This information is incorporated in the report with a descriptive summary and a preliminary evaluation. St Lucia had only three outgoing flights per week which was the lowest of all the islands considered, even tiny Montserrat having nine. Port facilities at Castries, despite the good natural harbour, were also considered to be very poor.

Road map of St Lucia.
See item no. 23.

Employment, Labour and Trade Unions

385 **A discussion on the needed inputs to foster employment generation in Barbados and LDCs.**
B. Meredith Burke.   Washington, DC: USAID, 1979. 79p.
This work is based on interviews with civil servants, bankers, management trainers and business people in St Lucia, Barbados, Antigua and St Kitts. The consensus was that the prime obstacle to viable business growth was the scarcity and low quality of human resources for business training. Difficulties in obtaining credit were another problem.

386 **Trade unions and women workers in the Eastern Caribbean.**
Cecilia Green.   *Voices of the African Diaspora*, vol. 7, no. 2 (1991), p. 30-34.
Conclusions based on interviews with seventeen trade-union personnel in five islands, including St Lucia, addressing the response of the unions to the problems and needs of women workers.

387 **Labour in the West Indies: the birth of a workers movement.**
Arthur Lewis, afterword by Susan Craig.   London, Port of Spain: New Beacon Books, 1977. 104p.
First published in 1939 as a Fabian society pamphlet immediately after the wave of strikes and workers' insurrections which spread throughout the English-speaking Caribbean just before the Second World War. As a result of this labour rebellion against colonialism the Caribbean Labour Congress was formed in 1945. The photographs, many of which come from the personal archives of Richard Hart, show that out of this upheaval came the organizations and the individuals who led the region for the next fifty years. St Lucia is described as politically one of the quietest islands as its Representative Government Association was long moribund.

388 **Gender roles in Caribbean agricultural labour.**
Janet Henshall Momsen.   In: *Labour in the Caribbean.*   Edited by
Malcolm Cross, Gad Heuman.   London; Basingstoke, England:
Macmillan Caribbean, 1988, p. 141-58. bibliog.

Looks at the gender division of labour under slavery and with free labour, discussing
gender divisions of task and labour time for both plantation labour and small farm
work in St Lucia. A woman's work depended on her partner's economic status and the
age of her children but women usually worked longer hours than men.

389 **Statement on the strike situation in the sugar valleys.**
St Lucia Sugar Association Ltd.   Castries: The Voice Publishing
Company, 5 April 1957. 6p.

Reports on the Sugar Workers Union complaint that payment by task meant that sugar
workers earned less than the minimum wage. The Association agreed to an increase in
wages and the setting up of a Commission of Enquiry.

Statistics

390 **Agricultural statistical digest 1984: St Lucia.**
Agricultural Statistical Unit. Castries: Ministry of Agriculture, 1985.
70p.
Divided into eight sections, this digest covers crop, livestock and fishing output, trade and credit plus ecology for the period 1980 to 1984.

391 **Caribbean statistical digest: social statistics: recueil statistique de la région Caraïbe: statistiques sociales.**
Caribbean Commission. Port of Spain, Trinidad: Central Secretariat, Caribbean Commission, vol. 3, no. 1, 1956. 119p. map.
Statistics covering education and culture, hospitalization and social security are given for the early 1950s.

392 **Statistical abstract to the Conference on the demographic problems of the area served by the Caribbean Commission.**
Caribbean Commission. Port of Spain, Trinidad: Caribbean Commission, Central Secretariat, Statistical Unit, 1957. 89p.
Provides information for St Lucia on population by age, marital status, sex and economic activity from the 1946 census with estimates for mid-1955. Birth and deathrates, marriage rates, and divorce and migration figures are given for each of the years 1935 to 1955.

393 **Caribbean plan: annual report 1963.**
Caribbean Organization. Hato Rey, Puerto Rico: Caribbean Organization, Central Secretariat, 1964. 143p.
Basic economic data for 1960 is provided in the form of comparative statistical tables for the member and observer countries of the Caribbean Organization. There is no

discussion of St Lucia's Development Plan but data is provided for the country's trade, manufacturing, roads, tourism, agriculture and population.

394   **1980-81 population census of the Caribbean: St Lucia.**
CARICOM Secretariat.   Kingston: Statistical Institute of Jamaica,
Printing Unit, 1984. 3 vols.

The Census was taken on 12 May, 1980. Volume one has a copy of the census forms and simple tabulations for the use of the government and general public. The second volume provides parallel coverage to that in the first volume but gives additional cross-tabulations of the data. Volume three includes preliminary tables, a brief commentary on the data and a comparison with population statistics for 1960 and 1970. It shows that St Lucia was growing faster than any other Eastern Caribbean territory despite net outmigration.

395   **St Lucia census report, 1891.**
Colonial Office.   London: HMSO, [n.d.]. 18p.

A report of the census conducted on 5 April 1891, which recorded 20,461 males and 21,759 females. Surprise is expressed at the loss of large numbers of men to Panama and the decline in the birthrate. Other early census results may be of interest and can be found in: *Census of St Lucia, 1871* (Castries: Government Printing Office, 1871. 11p.), the first published population census; *Census of St Lucia, 1881* (Castries: Government Printing Office, 1883. 12p.); *Report on the census of St Lucia taken on 7th April, 1901* (St Lucia Registrar's Office. Castries: Government Printing Office, 1901. 18p.), also published in the *St Lucia Gazette* (vol. 70, p. 907-24); *Report on the census of the island of St Lucia taken on the 2nd April, 1911* (St Lucia Registrar's Office. Castries: Government Printing Office, 1912. 68p.); *Report on the census of the Colony of St Lucia taken on 24th April, 1921* (St Lucia Registrar's Office. Castries: Government Printing Office, 1921. 61p.); and *West Indian census, 1946. Vol. 2, part H: census of the Windward Islands: Dominica, Grenada, St Lucia and St Vincent, 9th April, 1946* (Kingston: Government Printer, 1949. 79p.).

396   **Final report on the 1986 census of agriculture of St Lucia.**
David Demarque, Director of Agriculture.   Castries: Ministry
of Agriculture, Lands, Fisheries and Cooperatives, June 1987.
25p.

The number of farms on the island increased from 10,938 in 1973 to 11,551 in 1986 despite the fact that the amount of agricultural land had decreased at an annual rate of 1.5 per cent since 1961. The number of large farms had decreased because of housing and industrial development. The number of landless holdings had increased mainly in the drier northern and southern tips of the island because of an increase in livestock production especially poultry and pigs. Male farmers made up seventy-five per cent of the total. Earlier census results can be found in *West Indian Census, 1946. Vol. 1, part B: census of agriculture in Barbados, the Leeward Islands, the Windward Islands and Trinidad and Tobago* (Kingston: Government Printer, 1950. 74p.) and *West Indies census of agriculture, 1961: report on the Eastern Caribbean* (British Development Division in the Caribbean. Bridgetown, Barbados: British Development Division, 1968. 275p.).

397 **Annual Statistical Digest, 1968.**
Government of St Lucia. Castries: Development Planning and
Statistics, Premier's Office, 1969. 65p. annual.

Presents a tabulation of rainfall for 1955-68, births and deaths in 1966-68, transport
including traffic accidents, passenger movement and employment for 1963-68,
employment, finance, banking, trade, prices, teachers and pupils, and crime. The
number of cars and trucks registered doubled between 1962 and 1968 but the number
of road accidents only increased by fourteen per cent.

398 **Annual Statistical Digest, 1970.**
Government of St Lucia. Castries: Development Planning and
Statistics, Premier's Office, 1971. 77p.

The annual includes tables of rainfall for 1955-69, population and vital statistics in
1966-70, motor vehicles registered 1964-70, ships and cargo, passenger arrivals and
departures, employment, industrial production, forests, public finance, remittances,
banking, overseas trade 1962-70, prices, education and crime.

399 **Annual Statistical Digest, 1971.**
Government of St Lucia. Castries: Development Planning and
Statistics, Premier's Office, 1972. 89p.

Presents a collection of tables covering rainfall (1956-71), passenger arrivals and
departures (1965-71), employment (1966-71), industrial production (1964-71), public
finance, remittances, banking and overseas trade (1964-71), retail prices (1970-71),
number of school pupils (1960-71) and prisoners (1962-71). The table of remittances
shows that the dominance of the United Kingdom as a source of income steadily
declined after 1961 and by 1971 almost as much money was sent to St Lucia from
other countries as from the UK.

400 **Annual Statistical Digest, 1977.**
Government of St Lucia. Castries: Ministry of Trade, Industry and
Tourism, Department of Statistics, 1979. 59p.

Includes seventy-three tables covering meteorology, population (based on the 1970
census), agriculture (based on the 1973 agricultural census), forestry, industrial
production, energy, transport, trade, banking and finance, education, health, justice
and housing. In the decade 1966-67 to 1976-77 the number of primary schools
increased from sixty-three to seventy-six and the number of secondary schools from
three to eleven.

401 **Saint Lucia: report on the 1970 population census.**
Government of St Lucia. Castries: Census Office,
December 1970. 8p.

The preparation for and the carrying out of the 1970 census in March and April is
described in this brief account and preliminary returns of population are provided. The
total population for 1970 was enumerated as 101,064 compared to 86,108 in 1960. A
description of the enumeration districts and a population count for each district for 1960
and 1970 is included. Also of interest is the *Population Census of the Commonwealth
Caribbean, 1970: St Lucia* (Mona, Jamaica: University of the West Indies).

402 **Study of the agricultural sector of the OECS: country profiles on: Antigua, British Virgin Islands, Dominica, Grenada, Montserrat, St Kitts/Nevis, St Lucia, St Vincent.**
Francis A. Henry. Roseau: Organization of Eastern Caribbean States, Agricultural Diversification Unit, 1991. 177p.
A compilation of agricultural statistics from the eight member countries of the OECS.

403 **Statistical pocket digest, 1984.**
Organization of Eastern Caribbean States (OECS), Economic Affairs Secretariat. Antigua: OECS Printery, 1984. 18p.
Contains thirteen tables on the climate, population, health, education, leisure, tourism, transport, trade, energy, prices, national accounts, finance and banking for 1981 and 1982. The territories covered are Antigua and Barbuda, Montserrat, St Kitts-Nevis and the Windward Islands. Data is complete for St Lucia except for the numbers of medical personnel.

404 **An abstract of West Indian banana statistics (with special reference to the Windward Islands).**
Bishnodat Persaud. Cave Hill, Barbados: University of the West Indies, Institute of Social and Economic Research (Eastern Caribbean), 1966. 62p. (Statistical Series, no. 3).
This report was put together at a time of competition between Jamaica and the Windwards in banana production so it includes information on both major producers. Some forty-seven tables covering rainfall, land use, input levels, yields, wage rates, production, prices and distribution costs are included for the period 1950 to 1965.

405 **Population census of St Lucia, 1960: volume II.**
Population Census Division. Port of Spain, Trinidad : Central Statistical Office, Population Census Division, 1963. 208p.
The introduction to this volume provides explanatory notes and definitions used. The twenty-four summary tables cover information on households, age, race, religion, migration, education levels, marital status, fertility and union status, and the labour force as of 7 April 1960. Supplementary information can be found in *Eastern Caribbean population census, 1960: St Lucia summary tables* (Population Census Division. Port of Spain: Central Statistical Office, 1963. 208p.) and *Eastern Caribbean population census, 1960. St Lucia parts A and F: individuals by type of household and educational attainment. Parts B, D, E and G: marital status and union status; age, ethnic origin and religion; households and families; working population* (Population Census Division. Port of Spain: Central Statistical Office, 1969. 131p., 293p.).

Caribbean tourism statistical report: 1991 edition.
See item no. 94.

Intra-Caribbean trade statistics: statistiques du commerce intercaraïbe.
See item no. 280.

Meat production and consumption statistics of the Commonwealth Caribbean.
See item no. 494.

Environment

Urbanization and urban planning

406 **Urbanization and urban growth in the Caribbean: an essay on social change in dependent societies.**
Malcolm Cross. Cambridge, England: Cambridge University Press, 1979. 174p. map. bibliog.
Gives a sociological overview of the economy, political development and urban structure of the nations of the Caribbean region. Many tabulations of data are provided, in which information on St Lucia is included. Topics covered are the economic order, population structure and change, social structure and organization, race, class, education and politics. The conclusion considers the links between development and urban growth in the various territories of the region.

407 **The significance of a market in a Caribbean town – the case of Castries.**
Kenko Inoue. In: *Social and festive space in the Caribbean: comparative studies on the plural societies of the Caribbean.* vol. 2. Edited by Masao Yamaguchi, Masao Naito. Tokyo: Tokyo University of Foreign Studies, Institute for the Study of Languages and Cultures of Asia and Africa (ILCAA), 1987, p. 1-24.
Reports on fieldwork from August 1985 to February 1986. The marketplace itself is described as well as the types of vendors and customers, wares sold and interaction between people.

408 **Urbanization dynamics in the eastern Caribbean: focus on the Windward Islands.**
L. Ishmael. *Cities,* vol. 8, no. 3 (1991), p. 174-92.
The 1980s have seen unprecedented increases in the size of towns in the Windwards. Problems of growth have been exacerbated by structural, macroeconomic constraints, restricting the ability of local economies to expand sufficiently to provide employment opportunities and higher standards of living for local populations. Social and economic problems, land use conflicts and environmental degradation are readily identifiable in Roseau, St Georges, Kingstown and Castries.

409 **Sustainable development planning for Third World communities: a Caribbean case study.**
Edwin Joseph MacLellan. PhD thesis, University of Waterloo, Ontario, 1991. bibliog. (Available from University Microfilms International, Ann Arbor, Michigan, order no. DA NN67446).
High rates of urbanization in developing countries are posing major environmental problems for cities. Five case-studies of shantytown and inner city communities in Kingston, Jamaica provide information on the stresses and felt needs in these communities. The profile of the Kingston communities is supplemented by the experience from a St Lucia shantytown project.

410 **The human settlements of St Lucia.**
OAS. Washington, DC: General Secretariat of the OAS, 1988. 62p. maps.
This report stems from a three-year study by the Department of Regional Studies of the OAS. It includes a compilation of information about the geographical distribution of the rural population of St Lucia. The demographic size, infrastructure, and services of each settlement were surveyed and data is presented in cartographic (1:50,000 scale) and tabular form.

411 **Concentration and dispersal of settlements: Martinique and St Lucia.**
Romain Paquette. MA thesis, McGill University, Montreal, 1965. maps. bibliog.
The focus of this thesis is a comparison of settlement patterns in St Lucia and Martinique. It describes the location and growth of Castries, Vieux Fort and Gros Islet and the difficulties of developing the road system. It also includes a map of 1964 urban land use in Castries and a list of numbers and types of houses and commercial establishments.

412 **Vieux Fort, St Lucia master plan study.**
J. R. Petrie. Toronto: Project Planning Associates Ltd., 1970. 220p. maps.
The main objective of the study was to provide a second major urban centre in St Lucia complementary to the existing capital city of Castries. It was envisaged that this new centre would provide a growth pole in the south of the island. Development was to be based on industrial production for export and the expansion of tourism

encouraged by the building of new hotels. More tourist demand would stimulate domestic agricultural production which was seen as an essential part of the development strategy.

413 **Urbanization and planning in the Third World: spatial perceptions and public participation.**
Robert B. Potter. London: Croom Helm; New York: St Martin's Press, 1985. 284p. maps. bibliog.

Aimed at providing an overview of urbanization trends in the Third World this book is based on empirical work in Barbados, Trinidad and Tobago and St Lucia. The development and structure of Caribbean settlement patterns are described and the history of town planning and the housing structure of Castries are discussed in detail.

414 **Urbanization in the Third World.**
Robert B. Potter. Oxford: Oxford University Press, 1992. 48p. (Contemporary Issues in Geography Series).

This slim volume is aimed at senior high school students and presents the major themes necessary for an understanding of urbanization in the Third World. Unfortunately, the tables are based on information that is a decade or two old and this diminishes the utility of the book. The exercises on housing conditions use field data from Castries, St Lucia.

Housing

415 **Aspects of housing in the Caribbean.**
Caribbean Commission. Port of Spain, Trinidad: Caribbean Commission, Central Secretariat, 1951. 236p. tables. bibliog.

Provides data on urban and rural housing size, the number of occupants and amenities in the area. There is also a table listing slum clearance in Canaries and Castries in 1949 and public and private housing built in 1949-50 and under construction.

416 **The quality of housing in Grenada, St Lucia and St Vincent: a cartographic and statistical analysis.**
Robert B. Potter. London: University of London, Royal Holloway and Bedford New College, 1990. 31p. maps. (Papers in Geography, no. 7).

In this preliminary report on a major research project on housing quality, it is shown that St Lucia has the worst housing of the areas studied. Information from the 1980-81 censuses and eight variables of housing quality are mapped. Only in Castries do a majority of houses have electric light and gas for cooking. Houses are oldest in the south and along the leeward coast of St Lucia.

417 **A note concerning housing conditions in Grenada, St Lucia and St Vincent.**
Robert B. Potter. *Bulletin of Eastern Caribbean Affairs*, vol. 16, no. 4-5 (1990), p. 13-23. bibliog.

The initial findings of a two-year project involving the collection and analysis of housing systems' data from Grenada, St Vincent and St Lucia are presented here. Included are a comparative analysis and composite indices of housing disamenity.

418 **An analysis of housing in Grenada, St Lucia and St Vincent and the Grenadines.**
Robert B. Potter. *Caribbean Geography*. vol. 3, no. 2 (Sept. 1991), p. 107-25. maps.

Potter presents the initial findings based on statistical analysis of the diagnostic housing variables from the 1980-81 Census of the Commonwealth Caribbean. It was shown that St Lucia had a slightly poorer overall stock of houses than St Vincent and Grenada although it does have the highest proportion of houses rented from the government. In St Lucia seventy-four per cent of houses are built of wood, forty-one per cent are dependent on a standpipe for water, fifty-one per cent have a pit latrine and only forty-one per cent have electric lighting. Maps show the regional pattern of houses built before 1960 and the percentage of houses with a pit latrine toilet in St Lucia. Maps of factor scores indicate that general housing conditions in 1980 were highest in Castries and its surrounding suburbs.

419 **The new plan for Castries, St Lucia.**
J. C. Rose, A. C. Lewis. Castries: Office of the Executive Architect, Windward Islands, 1948. 31p. maps.

This is a new survey of Castries following the fire of 19-20 June 1948, which destroyed 522 residences and made 2,085 people homeless. The report contains a post-fire survey of land use, zoning and traffic circulation in Castries and proposes the redevelopment of over twenty acres in the centre of the town. Much of the former housing was overcrowded according to a 1945 survey. The draft town planning scheme emphasizes the need to group commercial areas and suggests the development of a new traffic pattern and car parks.

Natural resources

420 **Forestry in the Windward Islands.**
J. S. Beard, Development and Welfare in the West Indies.   Barbados: Advocate Co. Ltd., 1944. 183p. (Bulletin no. 11).

The section on St Lucia (p. 86-114) provides a general description of the island and of its forest policy. Beard recommends surveying the unescheated forest lands in order to reduce squatting and then establishing forest reserves. Botanical collections should be undertaken and sustainable management of the forest reserves, including the planting of sixty acres a year in trees, started. Trade in timber and timber products for the years

1934-42 shows a net deficit after 1939. The appendices list botanical names of species mentioned in the Report and drafts of the proposed new Forest and Crown Lands Ordinance.

421   **St Lucia's major potable water project.**
Caribbean Development Bank.   *CDB News,* vol. 7, no. 4 (Oct.-Dec. 1989), p. 6-7.

Notes that at the time of writing St Lucia had just begun work on the biggest water supply project in its history. A dam and reservoir are to be constructed on the middle reaches of the Roseau river which will provide adequate water for the next twenty years. Funding is to come from the Caribbean Development Bank, the World Bank, The Canadian International Development Agency and the Organization of Petroleum Exporting Countries. Care is to be taken during construction that environmental damage is minimized, for instance by reducing noise during the breeding season of the St Lucia Parrot.

422   **Survey of water supplies in the Caribbean.**
Caribbean Economic Review, vol. 1, nos. 1-2 (Dec. 1949), p. 43-79.

Reports on the state of water supplies in the late 1940s in the Caribbean. Shortly before the 1948 fire in Castries a new drinking water supply and sewage system and modern water treatment plant had been designed for the town. Vieux-Fort had been supplied with drinking water by the nearby United States Base since 1945 but with the deactivation of the Base the Colonial Government took over the Base water system and extended it to serve other communities within a ten-mile radius. Most major rural communities were supplied with piped drinking water which was filtered but not chlorinated. Irrigation using gravity flow from nearby rivers enabled the production of 160 acres of rice near Vieux-Fort in 1948. See also *Water in our development* (Caribbean Research Centre [St Lucia]. Castries: Caribbean Research Centre, 1980. 25p. maps) which was published in preparation for an experimental environment education project on the theme of water as part of the Eastern Caribbean Natural Area Management Programme. Also of interest is *Water supply situation in the LDCs of the East Caribbean at the beginning of the international drinking water supply and sanitation decade: a brief note* (Robert Goodwin. Port of Spain: CEPAL [Oficina para el Caribe], 1982. 17p.), which provides a description of the water situation in a number of East Caribbean islands, including St Lucia.

423   **Forest utilization in Saint Lucia, British West Indies.**
W. G. Lang.   *Caribbean Forester,* vol. 15, nos. 3-4 (July-Oct. 1954), p. 120-23.

Lang presents the results of an eight-year government forestry programme and the status of three forest reserves on the island. The emphasis of the forest programme is on the production of building material. The report includes a list of wood types harvested and the general characteristics of each type of timber.

424   Forestry and timber trees, St Lucia, B.W.I.

W. G. Lang.   Castries: Government Printer, 1955. 21p.

The area of high forest controlled by the Crown in 1955 was approximately 15,000 acres with about twelve marketable trees per acre. Lang explains that half a million board feet of timber was extracted from these forests each year. Felling was by axe with manual extraction of the logs. Species which were easy to saw by hand were most heavily cut and reafforestation was limited to ten acres a year because of a shortage of funds. Information is included on logging permits, seasoning and preservation methods, tree planting, and the characteristics of the main timber trees of St Lucia.

425   The integration of marine space in national development strategies of small island states: the case of the Caribbean states of Grenada and St Lucia.

Carlyle L. Mitchell.   Halifax: Dalhousie Ocean Studies Programme, 1982. 241p. maps.

A case-study prompted by the Foundation for Reshaping the International Order (RIO), this investigates marine resources in light of the Law of the Sea Convention. The study examines the magnitude of resources made available as a result of newly established Exclusive Economic Zones (EEZs). It also seeks to develop strategies for the development of marine industries (fishing) and all other uses of the EEZs, namely sea transport and tourism. The study makes a strong case for regional co-operation in marine resource management.

426   The role of action research in addressing critical issues in very small nations.

David Morley, Paul Wilkerson.   *The Operational Geographer,* no. 6 (1985), p. 38-41.

The authors focus on two projects, one of which is energy conservation in St Lucia. They describe how, in 1982, twenty-five St Lucians worked with the external research team and then presented a set of concrete suggestions for policy alternatives to twenty key local decision-makers. The participants formed an NGO to continue to be active on energy issues. The government has also established an energy desk and is exploring alternative energy sources, energy issues are now included in the school curricula and there is greater emphasis on traditional fuels.

427   Not so hot for thermal power?

West Indies Chronicle, vol. 89, no. 1,522 (Nov.-Dec. 1974), p. 334.

Records the start of research into the geothermal potential of the Sulphur Springs at Soufrière. However, it was felt that by the time the project came on stream, its high cost would be offset by a fall in world energy prices, and that the project cost would then be disproportionate to St Lucia's energy needs. It was thought unlikely that the British Government would finance the project but that Venezuela might consider providing funding.

428 **Energy resources in a Third World microstate: St Lucia household energy survey.**
Paul F. Wilkinson. *Resources and Energy,* vol. 6, no. 3 (Sept. 1984), p. 305-28.

An energy balance study was undertaken to provide data for a national energy policy and later a national development plan. Wilkinson used a household energy survey based on a national sample of 358 households to compute average annual household energy consumption largely focusing on cooking fuels. His results suggest that the use of firewood and charcoal has been greatly underestimated and that most energy is provided by local forest resources. The survey also revealed the frequent inefficient use of fuels with great opportunities for savings through improved efficiency and the importance of cultural and institutional factors in changing energy technologies. It is concluded that increased national electricity production is the most costly method of meeting future energy needs.

Environmental protection

429 **St Lucia Country Environmental Profile, 1988.**
Caribbean Conservation Association and Island Resources Foundation. Barbados and St Thomas, US Virgin Islands: Caribbean Conservation Association and Island Resources Foundation, 1988. 389p. map.

Provides a detailed overview of the physical environment, natural resources, demography, and rural and urban environmental differences based predominantly on census and other data from the 1970s and 1980s. Information is also included on the amount of land in the various slope classes and on soil loss from erosion which is estimated at 18.88 tonnes per hectare per year on Northern and Eastern slopes, 25.17 tonnes in Canaries, Anse la Raye, Dennery and Laborie, 47.20 tonnes in Micoud and Soufrière and 62.94 in Choiseul.

430 **Antigua and Barbuda, Dominica, Grenada, St Lucia, St Kitts and Nevis, St Vincent and the Grenadines: country environmental profile.**
The Caribbean Conservation Association. Barbados: Caribbean Conservation Foundation; St Thomas, US Virgin Islands: Island Resources Foundation, 1991. 6 vols.

These are environmental profiles designed as guides for development planning and resource management. Specific environment and development topics are examined, including management of marine and terrestrial systems; parks and protected areas; wildlife; agriculture; and institutional capabilities.

431 **Coastal zone management.**
J. R. Clark. *Land Use Policy,* vol. 8, no. 4 (1991), p. 324-30. bibliog.
St Lucia is included, amongst others, as a case-study of a country which suffers from
storm and flood damage. It is concluded that the management of coastal zones by
controlling the type, density and location of coastal settlements while preserving the
natural landforms which take the brunt of the storms, could reduce damage.

432 **A report on a study of conservation and development requirements
for the southeast coast of St Lucia.**
Eastern Caribbean Natural Area Management Program. Bridgetown:
Caribbean Conservation Association, 1983. 107p. (ECNAMP Report,
no. 1).
This study provides background information and recommendations concerning the
conservation of and development requirements for the south-east coast of St Lucia. It
synthesizes needs and ideas identified by local resource users and other interested
parties. The report was prepared as part of a project carried out jointly by ECNAMP
and the Government of St Lucia. Proposals which were in the process of
implementation are identified.

433 **Compte-rendu de la mission à Sainte-Lucie.** (Account of the mission
to St Lucia.)
Jacques Fournet. Paris: Ministère de l'Agriculture/INRA-CRAAG,
1982. 17p.
Prepared as a report to the Eastern Caribbean Natural Area Management Program, this
brief account provides details on a botanic survey of the proposed Maria Islands'
Nature Reserve carried out by a botanist based in Guadeloupe. It includes a list of
species, ecological observations, local names and some recommendations for
herbarium collection and conservation.

434 **A survey of the Maria Islands' marine environments (Vieux Fort,
St Lucia).**
Maureen Hayes, Nigel Lawrence. Castries: ECNAMP, 1982. 24p.
This survey was undertaken by two biologists from the fisheries management unit as
part of the project for the establishment of the Maria Islands' Reserve. It includes
general data, the identification and description of habitats, present uses of the area and
recommendations for future use, including a proposed boundary for the Nature
Reserve.

435 **A conservation strategy for the Caribbean.**
IUCN Bulletin (special report), vol. 12, nos. 5-6 (May-June 1981), 16p.
maps.
The IUCN has created a strategy for the conservation of living marine resources for
the Caribbean in conjunction with several Caribbean governments and the World
Wildlife Fund. In this special report the International Union for the Conservation of
Nature is presented and the Caribbean Conservation Association described. The
preservation of green turtles and coral reefs is investigated.

436   **Coastal parks as development catalysts: a Caribbean example.**
R. A. Meganck.   *Ocean & Shoreline Management,* vol. 15, no. 1
(1991), p. 25-36.

The site of the proposed Pitons National Park comprises an area of 1,600 acres of
terrestrial and marine habitat south of the town of Soufrière. Establishment of the park
would create 400 permanent jobs and help to stabilize the local economy, including
the long-term viability of the local fishing industry through sustained management of
the reef systems. The government of St Lucia was also considering an alternative
proposal of a large hotel-casino complex for the same site.

437   **Environmental planning and popular participation in Barbados
and the Eastern Caribbean: some observations.**
Robert B. Potter.   *Bulletin of Eastern Caribbean Affairs,* vol. 11,
nos. 4-5 (1985), p. 24-30.

Stresses the importance of environmental and physical planning in small nations with
a narrow resource base and raises issues about the relationship between planners and
the public. These arguments are linked with the author's research in Barbados,
Trinidad and Tobago and St Lucia.

438   **Land conservation in small developing countries: computer
assisted studies in St Lucia.**
E. Rojas, R. M. Wirtshafter, J. Radke, R. Hoser.   *Ambio,* vol. 17, no. 4
(1988), p. 282-88.

A Geographic Information System (GIS) was constructed for St Lucia in order to
study the relationship between land use, land capability, and human settlements. An
overlay of land use with land capability shows the extent to which rural development
is sustainable over the long term. A shortage of good quality land forces farmers to
cultivate steep slopes with poor soil. Until St Lucia's urban-based economy grows
significantly, over-exploitation of hillside land can be expected to continue. The GIS
provided detailed information on specific locations and quantification of critical
trouble spots and may help in assigning priorities in future land conservation efforts.

439   **Solutions to the 'Tragedy of the Commons': Sea-urchin
management in St Lucia, West Indies.**
Allan H. Smith, Fikret Berkes.   *Environmental Conservation,* vol. 18,
no. 2 (1991), p. 131-36. map.

St Lucia has an over-fished near-shore area. Management strategies for important non-
fish species such as sea-turtles, conch and lobster have included combinations of
closed season, minimum size and weight limitations and the protection of egg-bearing
females. This article discusses the harvesting of sea urchins which is carried out by
free diving. Sea urchins were traditionally sustainably collected by family groups over
a two-month period but recently it has become a commercial activity attracting many
unemployed young people who gather all year round. Sea urchin egg populations were
severely affected by the 1979 and 1980 hurricanes and their recovery in 1983 was
followed by uncontrolled harvesting. This led the government of St Lucia to impose a
ban on harvesting in December 1987 for the protection of the remaining stocks.

440   **Conservation and development in St Lucia.**
Roger D. Stone.   *World Wildlife Fund Letter*, no. 3 (1988), 8p. map.
A joint project by the World Wildlife Fund and the Eastern Caribbean Natural Areas
Management Program on the island of St Lucia is working to develop community
activities that provide economic support while conserving the coastal environment.
Tighter controls are allowing the recovery of threatened marine populations while
providing employment opportunities.

441   **Environmental status report and guidelines for development:**
St Lucia part 1-7.
United Nations Development Programme Physical Planning Project-
St Lucia.   US Virgin Islands: Island Resources Foundation,1974. 24p.
maps.
Both the positive and adverse environmental impacts of development are listed here,
especially of the Pigeon Island, Rodney Bay project. The report also tabulates the
archaeological sites, historical buildings and monuments worthy of preservation.

442   **Preparing for the worst.**
United Nations Environment Programme.   *The Caribbean and West*
Indies Chronicle, vol. 99, no. 1,581 (Aug.-Sept. 1984), p. 17-18.
A disaster preparedness seminar held in St Lucia in 1979 recommended a series of
disaster prevention and preparedness measures which were adopted by twenty-four out
of the twenty-seven Caribbean governments in 1981 as the Caribbean Action Plan.
The article reviews the range of natural disasters affecting the region including
hurricanes, earthquakes and volcanic eruptions, soil and coastal erosion. It is hoped
that the regional co-operation underlying the Caribbean Action Plan will help to
mitigate the worst effects of these disasters.

The reptiles of the Maria Islands, St Lucia: report to the Eastern
Caribbean Natural Area Management Program (ECNAMP) and the
World Wildlife Fund.
See item no. 72.

Reptile conservation on the Maria Islands (St Lucia, West Indies).
See item no. 73.

The status and conservation needs of the terrestrial herpetofauna of the
Windward Islands (West Indies).
See item no. 74.

Pollution

443 Marine debris contamination of beaches in St Lucia and Dominica.
C. J. Corbin, J. G. Singh. *Marine Pollution Bulletin*, vol. 26, no. 6 (June 1993), p. 325-28. map.

Two recreational beaches on the west coast and one non-recreational beach on the east coast of St Lucia were surveyed for this study. Samples were collected monthly between January and December, 1991 and it was discovered that plastics were the main component of debris in St Lucia. This was particularly marked on the east coast beach where some of the glass and plastic bottles found originated from as far north as the United States.The most important factor influencing the level of debris on east and west coasts is the direction of the prevailing winds and ocean currents.

444 Tar ball survey of six Eastern Caribbean countries.
C. J. Corbin, J. G. Singh, D. D. Ibiebele. *Marine Pollution Bulletin,* vol. 26, no. 9 (Sept. 1993), p. 482-86. map. bibliog.

This survey collected 412 samples in six countries between 1987 and 1991 of beach pollution by petroleum hydrocarbons as tar balls. In St Lucia 132 samples were collected from east and west coast beaches and these revealed one of the lowest levels of pollution by tar balls in the region with only Dominica having a lower result.

445 Petroleum contamination of the coastal environment of St Lucia.
C. J. Corbin. *Marine Pollution Bulletin*, vol. 26, no. 10 (Oct. 1993), p. 579-80. map. bibliog.

Five open ocean sites and three bays on the west coast were sampled for evidence of dissolved and dispersed petroleum hydrocarbons (DDPHs). There was minimal contamination in the bays indicating that land based activities associated with bulk storage and transhipment or domestic marine activities were not currently affecting the marine environment. The open ocean sites, however, were subject to moderate but persistent levels of petroleum contamination probably caused by tanker ballast washings and other maritime traffic.

Education

446 Utilization, misuse and development of human resources in the early West Indian colonies from 1492 to 1845.

M. K. Bacchus. Waterloo, Ontario: Wilfrid Laurier University Press, 1990. 412p. bibliog.

Describes the influences on education in the West Indies before emancipation and in the immediate post-emancipation period. For St Lucia Bacchus notes the resistance of the Roman Catholic clergy to the introduction of non-Catholic schools. The first public school in St Lucia was established in 1828 by the Anglican church but was closed after two years because of lack of funds. The non-denominational Mico charity later started a primary school in St Lucia in 1838 but with the discontinuance of the Imperial grant in 1845 it closed. Education is seen as a greater problem in St Lucia than in any of the other islands.

447 Environmental education practice: a St Lucia case study.

Justine Nigale Burt. MEd thesis, Queen's University, Kingston, Ontario, 1993. 247p. bibliog. (Available from University Microfilms International, Ann Arbor, Michigan, order no. DA MM85137).

A study of environmental education practice based on the study of several environmentally active groups. Current trends are towards greater inter-group co-operation and more focus on community participation approaches.

448 Report to the Government of St Lucia on the development of vocational training.

A. Figueroa-Colon. Geneva: International Labour Organization, 1966. 56p.

The author notes that regional co-operation in training would be very beneficial and recommends that a vocational training planning body, facilities to upgrade the skills of the existing workforce and an apprenticeship scheme should be set up to provide basic workshop training.

449 **Fundamental, adult, literacy and community education in the West Indies.**
H. W. Howes.   Paris: UNESCO, 1955. 79p. (Educational Studies and Documents, no. 15).

Provides a review of the state of education in the countries served by the Caribbean Commission, focusing on facilities for and experience in general education and in the training of teachers. In the section on St Lucia it is recorded that several teachers have been conducting classes in an endeavour to reduce the high incidence of illiteracy which is estimated at forty-five per cent. Howes points out that there is a demand for these classes but that teachers are handicapped by a lack of suitable teaching materials. It is suggested that a 'radio school' would be one solution.

450 **Vocational training: report to the government of St Lucia on the development of vocational training.**
International Labour Organization.   Geneva: International Labour Organization, 1964. 57p.

A review of the economic situation and existing training facilities in schools and apprenticeship schemes and recommendations for setting up a vocational training council and secretariat to establish vocational guidance and training standards.

451 **Environmental education practice: a St Lucian case study.**
Eva Krugly-Smolska.   MEd thesis, Queen's University, Kingston, Ontario, 1993. bibliog.

The author attempts to document environmental education in St Lucia. Each environmentally active group studied constituted a unit of analysis and multiple group involvement and shared responsibility was identified. The current trend is toward greater co-operation among active groups, with community participation approaches gaining in popularity.

452 **Educational program development approaches associated with Eastern Caribbean extension programs (Dominica, Grenada, St Lucia, St Vincent).**
Lorilee R. Sandmann.   PhD thesis, University of Wisconsin-Madison, Wisconsin, 1989. bibliog. (Available from University Microfilms International, Ann Arbor, Michigan, order no. DA 8916444).

A randomly selected sample of thirty-six agricultural extension officers from the four islands provided the data source using semi-structured interviews. The data suggested five categories of programme-development approaches: transactive; personal; institutional; clientele; and residual. Neither the subject's demographic background nor the level of professionalization were accurate predictors of the approach chosen.

453 **Youth unemployment in St Lucia, the West Indies: perceptions and expectations on education and work.**
Mary-Ellen Seaver-Taylor. PhD thesis, University of Illinois at Urbana-Champaign, 1987. (Available from University Microfilms International, Ann Arbor, Michigan, order no. DA 8803197).
This study compares and contrasts the views of two dominant actor groups, teachers and students, in Castries in 1982. The findings suggest that the extent to which St Lucian schools serve the needs of the modern formal labour market is exaggerated. The study showed that social struggles over occupational positions in which godfathers and relatives bargain for jobs may play a more important role than educational planning in solving youth unemployment.

454 **Fisheries Training School in St Lucia.**
G. T. Taylor. *The Caribbean,* vol. 14, no. 3 (March 1960), p. 51-52.
A Fisheries Training School was proposed for the Windward Islands in 1954. Taylor reports that only St Lucia carried out the original recommendations and the school was opened in 1959. It had three instructors, dormitories for sixteen students, workshops and a classroom. Sturdy open skiffs, measuring thirty feet in length, and powered by diesel engines were built at the school. These were then sold to the students on generous hire purchase terms. Such boats equipped with modern fishing gear enabled fishermen to be much more productive than they could be in the traditional Carib Canoe.

455 **Participatory approaches to development in St Lucia, West Indies.**
Carolyn Rachel Trist. MS thesis, University of Pennsylvania, Philadelphia, Pennsylvania, 1986. bibliog.
Reviews the implementation of the National Literacy Project which was started in 1984 to overcome the forty-six per cent illiteracy in the segment of the population over the age of fifteen, approximately 30,000 people. The other major project considered is the South-east coast Integrated Resources Management Project which drew local resource users such as fishermen and charcoal producers and also school children into discussions concerning the necessity for protecting the environment. Several other participatory groups have been established, such as Mothers and Fathers Groups and Backyard Farming Groups. Because of the unusually high level of illiteracy and the widespread use of Creole it was felt that non-conventional meetings and non-verbal communication were often most successful in St Lucia.

456 **Publications of the International Environmental Education Programme.**
United Nations Environment Programme. *UNESCO-UNEP Environmental Education Newsletter,* vol. 9, no. 1 (March 1984), p. 1-9.
Eight International Environmental Education Programme publications are described in this article and the sub-regional workshop on teacher training in environmental education for the Caribbean is considered. The objectives of the workshop were to examine teacher training modules and explore ways of adopting these modules. An individual report on St Lucia is included.

Education

The early education of a Nobel Laureate in the West Indies.
See item no. 273.

W. Arthur Lewis: another view.
See item no. 276.

Literature

Literary history and criticism

457   Pulse: a collection of essays by St Lucian writers.
Edited by Kendel Hippolyte, Melchior Henry.   Castries: The Source,
1980. 43p.

This is a collection of eleven essays by five St Lucian writers: Harold Simmons; John
Blanchard; Robert Lee; and the two editors. The essays were written over the previous
three decades and their publication represents a post-independence cultural flowering
of the nation. All the essays look at the Amerindian and African roots of St Lucian
culture and the influence of French and British colonial rule although their viewpoints
range from the historical to that of literary criticism.

**458   West Indian literature as an expression of national cultures: the
literature of St Lucia.**
Patricia Ismond.   *World Literature Written in English*, vol. 29, no. 2
(1989), p. 104-15.

Focuses on the works of Derek Walcott and Garth St Omer and the seminal role
played in St Lucia's cultural life by Harry Simmons. The dominance of the Roman
Catholic Church to which ninety-five per cent of the population belong and which
controlled education until the 1970s, combined with the general poverty, defined the
island in colonial times and provided the image which emerges from the literature.
The core of primitive religion alongside the 'white imperial religion', and the
clandestine liaisons between white and black inhabitants highlighting the double
standards of the orthodox morality, are also the source of themes in the works of both
Walcott and St Omer. The conclusion reached is that Walcott sees the promise of the
region as one of renewal, a renewal which is synonymous with the process of
indigenization.

Derek Walcott

459 **Columbus at the abyss: the genesis of New World literature.**
Robert Bensen. *Jamaica Journal,* vol. 24, no. 3 (1993), p. 48-54.
map. bibliog.
Bensen surveys the dilemma of being trapped between the Old World and the New as
it appears in works by Jean Rhys, Alejo Carpentier and the St Lucian, Derek Walcott.

460 **The art of Derek Walcott.**
Edited by Stewart Brown. Dufour: Seren Books, 1991. 231p. bibliog.
An edited volume on Derek Walcott's achievements as a poet, playwright, cultural
commentator and artist. The following literary works are discussed: *25 poems;
Epitaph for the young; Poems; In a green night; The castaway; The gulf; Another life;
Sea grapes; Star-apple kingdom; The fortunate traveller; Midsummer; The Arkansas
testament;* and *Omeros.* Most of Walcott's essays and poems are seen as reflecting the
struggle against colonialism.

461 **Derek Walcott: selected poetry.**
Selected and annotated by Wayne Brown. Oxford: Heinemann
International, 1981. 142p. (Caribbean Writers Series, no. 15).
Containing an introduction and notes to the poems, this collection includes selections
from *In a green night, The castaway, The gulf, Another life, Sea grapes* and *The Star-
apple kingdom,* which focus on West Indian landscapes and imagery.

462 **Poetic identity in the New World: Anne Bradstreet, Emily
Dickenson, and Derek Walcott.**
Jane Britton Buchanan. PhD thesis, Tufts University, Medford,
Massachusetts, 1985. bibliog. (Available from University Microfilms
International, Ann Arbor, Michigan, order no. DA 8526846).
Traces the development of poetic identity in three New World poets, all of whom were
seen as outsiders. Outsider status, however, was an asset for Walcott. It is argued that
since the publication of *The Star-apple kingdom* (1979) Walcott has become
increasingly well known and his movement toward America between 1973 and 1984
played an important role in the growth of his poetic identity. This study is the first
comprehensive analysis of his poetry up to 1984.

463 **A terrible beauty is born: problems of identity in two Caribbean
poets.**
Monica Jeanne Espinosa. PhD thesis, University of California, San
Diego, 1987. bibliog. (Available from University Microfilms
International, Ann Arbor, Michigan, order no. DA 8811860).
Nicolás Guillén and Derek Walcott are both poets with similar historical and
geographical backgrounds. However, their individual responses are very different:
Guillén sees himself as a mulatto introducing a new wholeness, a synthesis of Africa
and Europe, while Walcott's vision is of himself as forever torn between Europe, the

Caribbean and an unknown Africa. This study interprets Guillén's poetry as a poetry of hope and faith while Walcott's poetry is viewed as being full of resignation and scepticism. Guillén defines West Indian problems in political and economic terms while Walcott sees them as cultural. It is suggested that the divisions between African and European and between metropolitan and colonial which characterize St Lucia underscore that sense of absence dominating Walcott's poetry.

464 From the Green Antilles.
Edited by Barbara Howes. London: Panther Books, 1971. 397p.

An anthology of Caribbean writers divided into English, French, Spanish and Dutch sections. The author sees West Indian writing as being influenced by the psychology of islands, the intimacy, and the tension between the desire to leave and the desire to stay. St Lucia is represented by Derek Walcott's poem 'Missing the sea', from *The castaway* which expresses one aspect of nostalgia for his birthplace.

465 Derek Walcott's 'Omeros': recovering the mythical.
James T. Livingston. *Journal of Caribbean Studies,* vol. 8, no. 3 (1992), p. 131-40.

The author discusses Walcott's book-length epic poem in light of mythical linkages. *Omeros* is one of the most successful and important examples of the 'literature of reconnection', bridging the gap between the African and New World experiences.

466 Nationalism, nation and ideology.
Roberto Marquez. In: *The modern Caribbean.* Edited by Franklin W. Knight, Colin A. Palmer. Chapel Hill, North Carolina; London: University of North Carolina Press, 1989, p. 293-40.

Marquez uses Derek Walcott's writings, with their emphasis on a shared history, isolation and ethno-class confrontation, to provide a framework for a review of the literature of the Spanish-, French- and English-speaking Caribbean.

467 Caribbean vision: Derek Walcott and the post-racial civilization.
Colbert Nepaulsingh. *Writers, The Newsletter of The New York State Writers Institute,* vol. 2, no. 3 (spring 1989). Reprinted in *Caribbean Studies Newsletter,* vol. 19, no. 4 (fall 1992), p. 7.

Traces the influence of Dutch, English and Afro-Caribbean ancestry, the landscape of St Lucia and the mentorship of St Lucian intellectual and teacher, Harry Simmons, on Walcott's work.

468 Derek Walcott.
Edited by Rex Nettleford. *Caribbean Quarterly,* vol. 34, no. 4 (1992), p. 111-43. bibliog.

This issue celebrates the achievements of Nobel Prize winner Derek Walcott. It includes eleven poems, the play *Drums and Colors* (1962), an interview with the author, and tributes by Edward Baugh and Sir Philip Sherlock.

469 **The poetics and politics of "othering": contemporary African, African-American, and Caribbean drama, and the invention of cultural identities.**
Tejumola Olaniyan. PhD thesis, Cornell University, Ithaca, New York, 1991. bibliog. (Available from University Microfilms International, Ann Arbor, Michigan).

An examination of the black quest for cultural identity through works by Amira Baraka, Ntdzake Shange, and Nobel Laureates Wole Soyinka and Derek Walcott. One of the central themes of the study is institutional subordination and epistemological domination by a Eurocentric frame of reference.

470 **Derek Walcott's poetry: American mimicry.**
Rei Terada. Boston: North-eastern University Press, 1992. 260p.

Discusses the role of mimicry in Caribbean literature and views Walcott's cultural mimicry not as a problem but as a creative solution.

471 **African-Caribbean perspectives of worldview: C. L. R. James explores the authentic voice.**
Althea Veronica Trotman. PhD thesis, York University, Toronto, 1993. bibliog. (Available from University Microfilms International, Ann Arbor, Michigan, order no. DA NN84209).

C. L. R. James' discussion of the work of Derek Walcott, among other West Indian writers, is examined. He suggests that the literature of some Caribbean writers contains demonstrations of the presence of a worldview that speaks of liberation.

472 **Omeros.**
Derek Walcott. London: Faber & Faber; New York: Farrar, Straus & Giroux; Toronto: Collins Publishers, 1990. 325p.

Walcott's longest and most ambitious work to date, this clinched his award of the Nobel Prize for poetry. Based on the concept of Homer's Odyssey, the sufferings and adventures of Walcott's protagonists, the simple St Lucian fishermen Achille and Philoctete, take on the resonance of Greek mythology. St Lucian folk images, the island's landscape and the day-to-day dependence of farmers and fishermen on the vagaries of the weather are interwoven with observations on tourists and developers. Underlying this visible history is the interior unwritten epic of the pain of the exile.

473 **The Antilles: fragments of epic memory: The Nobel Lecture.**
Derek Walcott. New York: Farrar, Straus & Giroux, 1993. 34p.

Derek Walcott was awarded the Nobel Prize for Literature on 10th December, 1992. His Nobel Lecture is a stirring evocation of the multi-dimensional culture of the Caribbean. He uses the city of Port of Spain to illustrate these ideas. The lecture is a powerful re-envisioning of the themes that have enriched and informed his poetry. The book cover is illustrated by two of his watercolours.

The Arts

Visual arts

474   **Major exhibition for St Lucia-born artist.**
The West Indies Chronicle, vol. 86, no. 1,485 (Oct. 1971), p. 457.
Reports on an exhibition of work by the St Lucian-born artist, Llewellyn Xavier, at the
DM Gallery in London. His screen prints and lithographs, which deal with the life and
controversial death of George Jackson, one of the Soledad brothers, combine strong
poster-style visual images with extracts from letters. The artist sees his work as
creating a fusion between art and literature.

Festivals

475   **La Rose and La Marguerite societies in St Lucia.**
Daniel J. Crowley.   *Journal of American Folklore,* vol. 71, no. 282
(Oct.-Dec. 1958), p. 541-52.
Nearly every St Lucian belongs to one of two singing societies, the 'Roses' and the
'Marguerites'. The author reviews the history of these associations and explains the
significance of the groups in the current context of St Lucia's social structure. The
article describes and interprets the meaning of dances and songs performed by each
group.

476 **St Lucian carnival: a Caribbean art form.**
Raymond David Dunstan.   PhD dissertation, State University of New
York at Stony Brook, New York, 1978. bibliog. (Available from
University Microfilms International, Ann Arbor, Michigan, order
no. DA 7821848).

During eight months fieldwork in 1976-77, Dunstan followed the preparations for the
1977 carnival. Older informants who had witnessed the development of carnival over
many years were also interviewed. It was found that apart from the entertainment
aspects of the festivities, their social, economic, political and religious implications
were also significant. Carnival, as the major community celebration on the island,
provides a unique opportunity for the expression of national identity. It was felt that
carnival was most important, however, as a time when the creativity of individuals is
on public display and is critically judged according to local standards of beauty and
taste. The combined festival events constitute a spectacular, exuberant and culturally
significant St Lucian art form.

477 **Terre Bois Bois.**
Harold F. C. Simmons.   *Caribbean Quarterly*, vol. 6, no. 4 (1960),
p. 282-85.

The author describes the custom of 'Terre Bois Bois' which takes place in the area of
Choiseul on Ash Wednesday. The ceremony culminates in the burial of a stick figure,
an effigy constructed especially for this occasion. Simmons contends that the practice
is a 'fragmentary survival of Carnival'. The account includes the lyrics from three
songs sung at the ceremony.

Music and dance

478 **Musical events in the lives of the people of a Caribbean island,
St Lucia.**
Jocelyne M. Guilbault.   PhD thesis, University of Michigan, Ann
Arbor, 1984. bibliog. (Available from University Microfilms
International, Ann Arbor, Michigan, order no. DA 8422240).

An ethnomusicological study of St Lucian musical events and their cultural
implications, this includes detailed descriptions of the most common types of such
events: the seances of the La Rose and La Marguerite organizations; debut evenings,
full moon gatherings and beach parties; kwadril evenings; and wake celebrations.
Guilbault discussses the form and content of each musical event with their
characteristic melodies, associated gestures and movements and historical associations
and the web of relationships between musical genres in St Lucia.

479 **On interpreting popular music: zouk in the West Indies.**
Jocelyne Guilbault. In: *Caribbean popular culture.* Edited by John
A. Lent. Bowling Green, Ohio: Bowling Green State University
Popular Press, 1990, p. 79-97.
Introduces the 'soundscape' of Martinique, Guadeloupe, Grenada, and St Lucia. The
author discusses the making of zouk music in a social and political context and the
music's impact on society.

Folklore

480 **Oral and folk traditions of Saint Lucia.**
Compiled by Joyce August. Castries: Lithographic Press, 1986. 39p.
(Cultural Heritage Series, no. 1).
This is a collection of articles based on selected interviews between teachers who
attended the oral tradition workshop and the residents of St Lucia. There is an oral
history of an eighty-year-old St Lucian woman emphasizing the festivals of St Lucia
and of Sessenne, the singer and Queen of Culture in St Lucia. Other oral information
is grouped together on topics such as the calabash, drumming, houses, woodworking
and rural life.

481 **West Indian sea magic.**
Jane Beck. *Folklore*, vol. 88 (1977), p. 194-202. bibliog.
St Lucian fishermen are believed by fishermen from other islands to use obeah to give
them their uncanny ability to catch fish. Using information supplied by a St Lucian
fisherman, the author describes the various potions and ceremonies employed to
ensure good fishing. It has also been said that too much obeah was used, resulting in
the fish spoiling very quickly.

482 **To windward of the land: the occult world of Alexander Charles.**
Jane C. Beck. Bloomington, Indiana; London: Indiana University
Press, 1979. 309p. bibliog.
Depicts the life history of a fisherman and obeah man of St Lucia and illustrates the
high mobility and flexible family structure of St Lucians. The second part of the book
concentrates on the folklore, including patois songs, traditional medicines·and magical
potions of the island. Detailed information is provided on the preparation and usage of
medicinal plants and botanical names are given where known.

483 **Naming customs in St Lucia.**
Daniel J. Crowley. *Social and Economic Studies,* vol. 5 (1956),
p. 87-92.
Crowley provides interesting details on naming customs in the island. He points out
that illegitimate children usually take the mother's surname. Catholic children have
three given names.

484 **'Do'en dee dance': description and analysis of the jombee dance of Montserrat.**
Jay D. Dobbin. PhD thesis, Ohio State University, Columbus, Ohio, 1982. bibliog. (Available from University Microfilms International, Ann Arbor, Michigan, order no. 8305318).
Traces the African roots of a trance ritual performed in Montserrat. It is thought to be similar to the Kele ritual of St Lucia.

485 **Research in ethnography and ethnohistory of St Lucia: a preliminary report.**
Edited by Manfred Kremser, Karl R. Wernhart. Horn-Vienna: Verlag Ferdinand Berger & Söhne, 1986. 170p. maps. bibliog. (Vienna Contributions to Ethnology and Anthropology, band 3).
Contains articles on the development of folk research in St Lucia, on the kélé tradition and ceremony, on traditional craft technologies, and on the ethnohistory of runaway slaves. This is the preliminary report of a joint research project undertaken by the Institute of Ethnography at the University of Vienna, the St Lucia Folk Research Centre and the National Research and Development Foundation between 1982 and 1986.

486 **Give me some more sense: a collection of Caribbean island folk tales.**
Jacintha A. Lee. London; Basingstoke, England: Macmillan, 1988. 67p.
Ten St Lucian folk tales are translated from patois and illustrated with black-and-white sketches. The hero of the stories is Compere Lapin, who is known as Brer Rabbit in English. These children's tales have been passed down by word of mouth in patois and are known as Tim-Tim stories.

487 **The kele (chango) cult in St Lucia.**
George Eaton Simpson. *Caribbean Studies,* vol. 13, no. 3 (Oct. 1973), p. 110-16.
The kélé ceremony in St Lucia resembles the Shango ritual in Trinidad and other similar Afro-Caribbean rites elsewhere in the region but the kélé belief system seems to be much simpler. The names of only two Yoruba deities, Sango and Esu, persist in St Lucia perhaps because no groups of post-emancipation immigrants from Africa settled there. The ceremony is undertaken to ask the African ancestors of the participants for protection and to give thanks for past favours received. Babonneau is the main centre of kélé and the ceremony utilizes polished Amerindian stone axes, drums and agricultural implements. A ram, and sometimes a cock, are sacrificed and their blood is drunk. No woman may observe the sacrificial act but they may take part in the ceremony by singing and dancing away from the site of the sacrifice.

Food and Drink

488 **A study of shark consumption patterns in the South-Eastern Caribbean.**

John E. Adams. *Cajanus,* vol. 22, no. 2 (1989), p. 85-109. bibliog.

This study examines shark meat consumption habits in Trinidad and Tobago, St Vincent and St Lucia.

489 **Fish lovers of the Caribbean.**

John E. Adams. *Caribbean Studies,* vol. 25, no. 1-2 (1992), p. 1-10.

A study of fish consumption patterns and preferences in 623 households in St Lucia, Trinidad and Tobago, St Vincent and Belize. The author finds a high level of fish consumption and acceptance of a greater range of fish varieties in the diets of Caribbean fish lovers.

490 **Vitamin E, lipid fractions and fatty acid composition of colostrum, transitional milk and mature milk: an international comparative study.**

E. R. Boersma, P. J. Offringa, F. A. J. Muskiet, W. M. Chase, I. J. Simmons. *American Journal of Clinical Nutrition,* vol. 53, no. 5 (May 1991), p. 1,197-204.

Triglycerides, cholesterol, fatty acid compositions and tocopherals were determined in colostrum, transitional milk and mature milk in St Lucia. With progress in lactation, there was an augmented synthesis of fatty acids in the mammary gland and a tendency for increase in fat-globule size as milk matures. Transitional and mature milks contained higher concentrations of components considered to be derived from the fat-globule membrane compared with those reported for Western countries. The proportion of medium-chain fatty acids in mature milk was two to three times higher than in developed countries.

491 **The pre-eminence of roots and tubers in the diets of the Caribbean peoples.**

Nigel Durrant. *The Courier,* no. 101 (Jan.-Feb. 1987), p. 89-91.

Durrant considers the importance of root crops which are staple food items among Caribbean peoples. Per capita production varies from island to island. St Lucians consumed 17.1 kilogrammes each but only produced 12.2 kilogrammes per capita in the early 1980s. Attempts to increase the production of root crops are receiving more official attention than previously in order to diversify agriculture.

492 **Plat Kweyol Ste Lucie and the digestive system.**

Marcella Edlay. Castries: The Voice Publishing Company, 1990. 112p.

The first half of this book contains information on dietary problems and diseases of the digestive system, Creole food composition, and on callaloo and healing plants and herbs of St Lucia. The second half offers recipes for Creole one-pot dishes including eighteen meatless dishes and twenty-six meat dishes. Recipes are also provided for a vegetarian Creole Christmas family menu.

493 **Food technology and the food industry in St Lucia, West Indies.**

H. H. Lubin. *Food Technology,* vol. 41, no. 9 (Sept. 1987), p. 151-53.

The current status of food technology and food industry activities in St Lucia is reviewed. Topics include: the agricultural dominance of bananas and coconuts; locally produced fats such as coconut oils, meat products, fish, fruits, vegetables and spices; current constraints on food processing; and the need for continuing institutional assistance from the British government. The co-operative nature of processing activities in St Lucian agro-industry is discussed.

494 **Meat production and consumption statistics of the Commonwealth Caribbean.**

J. M. Mayers with the assistance of H. W. Blades. Trinidad: University of the West Indies, Department of Agricultural Economics and Farm Management, 1970. 204p. (Occasional Series, no. 5).

Contains thirteen tables related to St Lucia. Topics covered include: meat imports (1935-47); the average value of meat imports (1959-67); average retail prices; net imports of various types of meat for the period 1956-1968; the number of animals slaughtered and local meat production (1956-67); and consumption of meat (1956-67).

Provision ground and plantation labour in four Windward Islands: competition for resources during slavery.

See item no. 131.

The national food and nutrition survey of St Lucia, 1974.

See item no. 196.

A food and nutrition policy for St Lucia with programmes for incorporation into the National Development Plan 1975-1980.

See item no. 197.

Mass Media

495 **Mass media in St Lucia.**
J. Laurence Day. In: *Mass media and the Caribbean.* Edited by
Stuart H. Surlin, Walter C. Soderland. New York: Gordon & Breach,
1990, p. 97-102. (Caribbean Studies, vol. 6).
An historical overview of the print and broadcast media as well as a brief account of
the social and political context of the island. The printed media are characterized by
private ownership and a libertarian orientation. Radio and television are a mix of
state-operated and privately funded stations. The author notes a dearth of research
regarding the emergence of Kweyol (French-based patois) in the media.

496 **The Voice of St Lucia.**
Castries: Voice Publishing Co. Ltd., 1885-
The oldest continuously published newspaper in the region, *The Voice* provides
national and regional news in St Lucia.

Directories, Yearbooks and Handbooks

497 The pocket guide to the West Indies.

Sir Algernon Aspinall.   London: Methuen, 1960. rev. ed. 474p. maps.

First published in 1907, this guide contains general information on the history, geology, climate, population, food and clothing of the region and provides further reading and detailed advice for the sea voyage to the West Indies. The section on St Lucia (p. 166-80), offers a description of the sites of various historical events, mainly naval battles against the French. Only five hotels are listed, all in Castries or Vigie. It is noted that the Castries Club is only open to men but extends a welcome to visitors with proper introductions. Overall the guide provides a glimpse of the region as it was just before the age of mass tourism.

498 1993 Caribbean Islands handbook.

Edited by Sarah Cameron, Ben Box.   Bath, England: Trade & Travel Publications; New York: Prentice Hall General Reference, 1992. 815p. maps. bibliog.

First published in 1988 this has become an annual publication for the traveller to the region. It contains general information on health, watersports and sailing, walking, responsible tourism, flora and fauna, pre-columbian civilizations, and economic indicator and climatic tables. General information for travellers as to visa requirements, money, language and local and international travel is also provided. A list of Caribbean festivals shows that St Lucia has more than any other island. The section on St Lucia on p. 499-520 includes a map of central Castries and provides useful information on flora and fauna and how to visit the nature reserves. The various festivals are described and good places to eat noted.

499   **The Cambridge encyclopedia of Latin America and the Caribbean.**
      Edited by Simon Collier, Thomas Skidmore, Harold Blakemore.
      Cambridge, England: Cambridge University Press, 1992. 2nd ed. 480p.
      maps.

A beautifully illustrated volume covering the physical environment, economy, people
and culture of the countries of the region. St Lucia is mentioned in relation to the
banana industry, its membership in CARICOM, independence and Walcott's
contribution to Caribbean literature.

500   **The Caribbean handbook: 1992/93.**
      Edited by Clayton Goodwin.   St John's, Antigua: FT Caribbean,
      1992. 236p. maps.

This is an annual publication aimed at the business traveller. It contains general
articles on the events of the political year, agriculture, aviation, shipping,
communications, tourism, and facts and figures for the business person. There is also a
chapter entitled 'a personal view of the West Indies' by John Figueroa which focuses
on the ethnic mix found in the region. The section on St Lucia (p. 173-79) focuses on
the business environment, infrastructure, the economy, communications and hotels
ranked according to their suitability for business meetings.

501   **Handbook and guide to St Lucia.**
      R. F. McHugh.   London: [n.p.], 1890. 58p.

The first half of the book provides an outline of the political history, population and
trade of the island. The landscape, soils, agriculture and major settlements of each
quarter are described. The book is clearly aimed at potential settlers indicating that
abandoned sugar estates can be purchased very cheaply and that ' all the land is fitted
for the cultivation of cocoa, nutmegs, spices, fruits and fibres' (p. 47).

502   **The St Lucia handbook, directory and almanac for the year 1924.**
      Compiled by W. Wells Palmer.   Castries: The Government Printing
      Office, 1924. 350p. map.

Provides a description of the history and geology of the island, and details on its
climate (with rainfall for 1890 to 1923), birds, trees and grasses found, the towns,
villages and roads, and the economic situation. Census population totals from 1769 to
1921 are also included along with a government and business directory and
information for visitors.

503   **St Lucia yearbook 1964.**
      The Voice.   Castries: The Voice Publishing Company, 1964. 96p.
      map.

This is the first such handbook of St Lucia published since 1924. It has a foreword by
the Administrator, Captain G. J. Bryan, and includes data on tourist attractions,
population, history, government, trade and finances, a trade directory and a local
'Who's Who'.

504 **The Windward Islands annual 1965.**
Letchforth, England: Letchforth Publishing Agency for the Windward
Island Governments, 1965. 60p.

Illustrated with black-and-white photographs, this annual contains articles on hotel
development, fruit production, telecommunications, insects, sharks, crabs, crayfish
and lobsters.

Bibliographies

505 **The catalogue of the West India Reference Library.**
Introduced by John Aarons.   Millwood, New York: Kraus
International Publications, 1980. 6 vols.

This catalogue of the Institute of Jamaica's West India Reference Library is organized in two parts: authors and titles (volumes one to three) and subjects (volumes four to six). Covering the period 1547 to 1975, the collection emphasizes regional works dealing with history, travel and description, government, economic and social conditions, literature, sugar, slavery, and African culture. Books and pamphlets are classified according to the Dewey system (with the exception of the fiction category), and periodicals are categorized by means of a modified Cutter system.

506 **West Indian literature: an index to criticism 1930-1975.**
Jeanette Allis.   Boston, Massachusetts: G. K. Hall, 1981. 353p.
bibliog.

A modified version of a University of the West Indies' MPhil thesis. The index is prefaced by an introductory essay which highlights the problems of the novelist in exile and the distinction between internal and external criticism. Part one comprises an index of authors with general evaluations and appraisals of specific works, while part two provides an index of critics and reviewers with references to their essays. There is also a chronological listing of articles and books on West Indian literature.

507 **A guide to records in the Windward Islands.**
E. C. Baker.   Oxford: Basil Blackwell for the University of the West
Indies, 1968. 95p. map.

Most of the early records of St Lucia were lost in fires which severely damaged Castries in 1796, 1927 and 1948. Deed record books are in French, at least in part, until 1898. The earliest records kept by the Chief Registrar date from 1807 and include court judgements, land titles and births, marriages and deaths. Copies of newspapers from 1885 are also preserved by the Chief Registrar. Documents in the Administrative Building, the Chief Minister's Office, Government House, Police

Headquarters. the Public Library, the Victoria Hospital, and Castries Mental Hospital are listed in this guide. The admission registers of several schools, a few records surviving in Castries and Soufrière Town Council Offices, and records from various churches, the St Lucia Archeological and Historical Society, the Co-operative Bank and five private individuals are identified.

508 **Publications and theses from the Bellairs Research Institute and the Brace Research Institute of McGill University in Barbados, 1956-1984.**
Holetown, Barbados: Bellairs Research Institute, 1984-85. 52p.

The Bellairs Research Institute concentrates on marine and terrestial biology with some geology and geography while the Brace Research Institute was concerned with the weather and climate and seawater desalination. This bibliography lists articles, reports and theses derived from work carried out at these two Institutes.

509 **Bibliography of women writers from the Caribbean 1831-1986.**
Brenda F. Berrian, Art Brock, Associate Editor. Washington, DC: Three Continents Press, 1989. 360p.

Creative works, novels, short stories, poetry, folklore, autobiographies, biographies and children's literature are listed in this bibliography. The work is divided into four sections by language and the entries are not annotated.

510 **Our ancestral heritage: a bibliography of the roots of culture in the English-speaking Caribbean.**
Compiled by Edward Brathwaite. Kingston: Savacou Publications, 1977. 194p.

A partially annotated bibliography prepared for Carifesta 1976. Subject areas include biographical references and studies, Caribbean background, the Amerindians, Europe, European settlement, plantations and planters, slavery, the European Church and missions in the Caribbean and African influences.

511 **Current Caribbean bibliography: cumulative issue 1954-58.**
Caribbean Commission. San Juan, Puerto Rico: Caribbean Commission, 1961. 90p.

Includes periodicals, government serials and monographs printed between 1954 and 1958 in the countries of the region associated with the United States, Britain, France and the Netherlands. There are no periodicals from St Lucia but St Lucian government serials cover legislative reports and reports from the Medical Department, the Ministry for Trade and Production, Customs, the Post Office, and the Registrar's Office. Nine monographs concerning St Lucia are included, of which three are plays by Derek and Roderick Walcott.

512 **The Caribbean 1975-1980: a bibliography of economic and rural development.**
Manuel J. Carvajal. Metuchen, New Jersey; London: The Scarecrow Press, 1993. 897p.

This bibliography emphasizes studies which have had an impact on the formulation of public policy related to economic and rural development in the Caribbean, excluding Cuba and Puerto Rico. Periodical publications, such as statistical bulletins and yearbooks, and technical publications are excluded. Annotations are provided wherever the topic is not clear from the title. The entries are divided into twelve geographical sections, with the section on the Smaller Territories of the Lesser Antilles further divided by territory. The sub-section on St Lucia contains forty-six entries of which four have brief annotations. The index covers persons, institutions, conferences, journal titles and works of corporate or uncertain authorship.

513 **Caribbeana 1900-1965: a topical bibliography.**
Lambros Comitas. Seattle, Washington; London: University of Washington Press for the Research Institute for the Study of Man, 1968. 909p. map.

Divided thematically into ten sections, this work covers: an introduction to the Caribbean; the past; the people; elements of culture; health; education and welfare; political issues; the environment and human geography; socio-economic activities and institutions; soils, crops and livestock; and economic and social prospects. Each section is subdivided into topics for a total of sixty-seven chapters with considerable cross listing. There are both author and geographical indices. Entries are not annotated. There are twenty-five references for St Lucia mostly relating to health issues.

514 **The complete Caribbeana 1900-1975: a bibliographic guide to the scholarly literature.**
Lambros Comitas. New York: KTO Press, 1977. 4 vols.

The most comprehensive bibliography for the region of books published until 1975. Topics relating to travel, history, demography and ethnic groups are covered in the first volume, while volume two includes references on cultural institutions, religion, language, health, education, housing and politics. The third volume covers economics, industries, the environment, human geography, soils, crops and livestock. In the final volume entries are listed by author and by territory.

515 **Bibliography of the West Indies (excluding Jamaica).**
Frank Cundall. Kingston: Institute of Jamaica; London: H. Sotheran, 1909. Reprinted, New York; London: Johnson Reprint, 1971, 1972. 179p.

Entries are listed country-by-country in chronological order of books, pamphlets and magazine articles some of which were held by the Institute of Jamaica of which Cundall was secretary. Unfortunately few of these unannotated entries are readily available today.

516 **More than sea water and sand: serials of the British Caribbean.**
Timothy Dodge. *Serials Review*, vol. 3 (1988), p. 43-52.

This is a short paper which provides details of twenty-nine currently published serials produced in the British Caribbean. Most of these have a circulation of under one thousand subscriptions.

517 **Geographic publications on Latin America during the 1960s: selected bibliography.**
Ernst Griffin, Clarence W. Minkel. Michigan State University, Department of Geography, 1970. 47p.

Described as being based on publications by United States geographers plus theses and dissertations, this in fact also includes work by geographers at Canadian Universities and other English-speaking geographers. The organization is by country and topic but entries are not annotated. There are three items on St Lucia.

518 **Caribbean writers: a bio-bibliographical-critical encyclopedia.**
Edited by Donald Herdeck. Washington, DC: Three Continents Press, 1979. 943p. map. bibliog.

A massive collection of approximately 2,000 authors and 15,000 works covering the English, French, Dutch and Spanish-speaking territories. The West Indian section is co-edited by John and Dorothy Figueroa; it provides a list of writers by country together with an alphabetical list of their lives and major works. Also included are bibliographies, critical studies, general anthologies, background books and selected journals.

519 **Caribbean topics: theses in Canadian University Libraries.**
Compiled by Theo L. Hills. Montreal: McGill University, Centre for Developing Area Studies, 1969. 13p.

An unannotated list of Master's theses and doctoral dissertations grouped by academic discipline and University. There are three entries on St Lucia.

520 **Dictionary of Caribbean biography.**
Edited by Ernest Kay. London: Melrose Press, 1969. 335p.

The information included in this dictionary is based on questionnaires sent to notable persons of the region, defined here as including all countries of the Caribbean Basin. There are approximately 3,000 entries.

521 **Agriculture in the economy of the Caribbean: a bibliography.**
Land Tenure Center Library. Madison, Wisconsin: Land Tenure Center, 1974. 87p. (Training and Methods Series, no. 24).

The social and political aspects of agriculture are covered in this volume as well as economic and development issues.

522 **Bibliography of Latin America 1955-1964.**
Compiled by Lois E. Mason.   Columbus, Ohio: Ohio State University,
Department of Geography, 1965. 232p.

The classification is by region and by topic and items in Spanish, Portuguese, French,
Italian and German are included as well as those in English. There are three entries on
St Lucia.

523 **A select bibliography of publications and studies relating to
Human Resources in the Commonwealth Caribbean.**
Marianne Ramesar.   Mona, Jamaica: Institute of Social and Economic
Research, 1981. 127p. (Human Resources, no. 3).

Covers social, economic and population issues for the Commonwealth Caribbean.

524 **Earthquake studies in the Caribbean: a bibliographic guide.**
Compiled by Lutishoor Salisbury, edited by Mary Vance.
St Augustine, Trinidad: Vance Publications, 1986. 40p.

A comprehensive listing of research on earthquakes documented in the Caribbean, this
guide was compiled by the librarian of the engineering and physical sciences division
of the University of the West Indies, St Augustine. The entries are arranged by
countries and within this order listed alphabetically by author.

525 **Women in the Caribbean: a bibliography.**
Bertie Cohen Stuart.   Leiden, the Netherlands: Royal Institute of
Linguistics and Anthropology, Department of Caribbean Studies, 1979.
163p.

Contains 631 entries from most Caribbean language areas plus a few items in German
and Portuguese. Partial annotations are in English. General bibliographies and those
covering individual women are followed by some introductory material and details of
women's organizations. The main part of the bibliography is divided into sections on
family and household, cultural factors, education, economics and politics and law.

526 **Women in the Caribbean: a bibliography: part two.**
Bertie Cohen Stuart.   Leiden, the Netherlands: Royal Institute of
Linguistics and Anthropology, Department of Caribbean Studies, 1985.
246p.

Intended as a supplement to the earlier volume, this bibliography contains titles from
1979 to 1985 along with earlier works omitted from the 1979 publication. The
arrangement follows the same format with the exception of a new section on the
creative arts and the deletion of women's organizations. This time names of publishers
are included. Some references are to unpublished student work and not all entries are
annotated.

527 **Bibliographic survey of Latin America and the Caribbean, 1969.**
United States Department of the Army. Washington, DC: US
Government Printing Office, 1969. 319p. maps. (DA Pamphlet 550-7).

This survey includes unclassified items on the open shelves of the Army Library, the
Adjutant General's Office, Army Headquarters. It covers literature published between
June 1964 and December 1968. The first sixty pages contain a review of social,
economic and political problems of the region, territorial disputes, national security
and the armed forces. This is followed by an annotated bibliography for the
independent countries and non-independent areas and regions. St Lucia is included in
the West Indies section. The map appendix includes a 1:4,942,080 map of the West
Indies produced by the National Geographic Society in 1968 with St Lucia inset at the
scale of twelve miles to the inch.

528 **Caribbean: a collection of dissertation titles 1861-1983 searched.**
University Microfilms International. Ann Arbor, Michigan:
University Microfilms, 1984. 84p.

Master's theses and doctoral dissertations are grouped by country and subject in this
publication. Topics covered are: accounting, agriculture, agronomy, American studies,
anthropology, archaeology, biology, botany, chemistry, demography, ecology,
economics, education, energy, engineering, entomology, fine arts, folklore,
geochemistry, geography, geological survey, geology, geophysics, health sciences,
history, home economics, hydrology, instruction, journalism, language and literature,
law, linguistics, library science, literature management, marine sciences, marketing,
mass communications, music, oceanography, palaeontology, philosophy, physical
physiology, political science, psychology, recreation, religion, social geography,
social work, sociology, speech, theatre, theology, urban and regional planning, and
zoology.

529 **To St Lucia, with love.**
Compiled by Robert V. Vaughn. Frederiksted, St Croix: Aye-Aye
Press, 1980. 49p.

Subtitled 'The bibliography of a library collection for the people of St Lucia upon
achieving independence presented by the people of the United States', the 380 titles in
this collection were given by the United States International Communication Agency
as the basis of a core collection housed at the Morne complex of the Teachers College,
Extra-Mural Department, University of the West Indies. The items in the collection
were selected by a Caracas-based Regional Library consultant and consist entirely of
fiction and non-fiction books in English published in the United States. This
unannotated bibliography was compiled from the order slips and despite attempts to
verify if books had actually been received in St Lucia, there remained some doubt as
to whether all books had been delivered. Entries are by both author and subject.

530 **Education in the Eastern Caribbean: a select bibliography.**
Audine Wilkinson. *Bulletin of Eastern Caribbean Affairs,* vol. 7,
no. 4 (Sept.-Oct. 1981), p. 36-44.

Comprises books, journal and newspaper articles, documents, pamphlets, conference
proceedings, official reports and theses. Most items deal with education in the general
region.

531   **Economic literature on the Commonwealth Caribbean: a select**
      bibliography based on material available in Barbados.
      Audine C. Wilkinson, Andrew S. Downes.   Cave Hill, Barbados:
      Institute of Social and Economic Research (Eastern Caribbean), 1987.
      503p. (Occasional Bibliography Series, no. 8).

The bibliography covers the literature up to 1986 and entries are not annotated. The main sections, each of which is sub-divided by topic and territory or region, are: general studies; models of Caribbean economy; economic development; planning and cost benefit analysis; national income accounting and input-output analysis; money, banking and finance; inflation; wages and incomes policy; fiscal theory; consumption, savings and investment; economic integration; international economics; agriculture; fisheries; industry, mining and energy; tourism; communications and transport; distribution and commerce; human resources; income distribution and poverty; population, migration and urbanization; and general reference works. Entries on St Lucia are grouped with those of the other Windward Islands.

Indexes

There follow three separate indexes: authors (personal and corporate); titles; and subjects. Title entries are italicized and refer either to the main titles, or to other works cited in the annotations. The numbers refer to bibliographical entry rather than page numbers. Individual index entries are arranged in alphabetical sequence.

Index of Authors

160

163

Index of Titles

Index of Subjects

Map of St Lucia

This map shows the more important towns and other features.

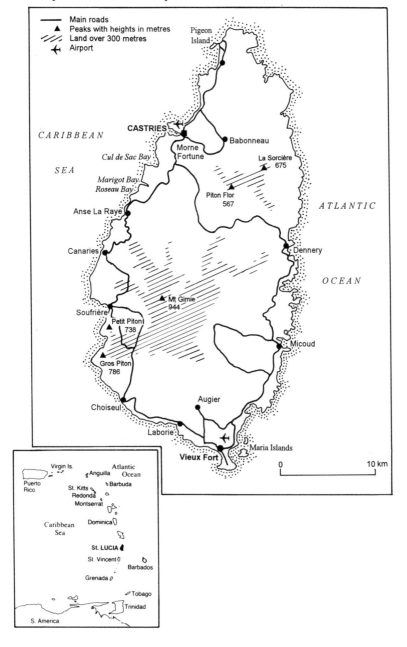

ALSO FROM CLIO PRESS

INTERNATIONAL ORGANIZATIONS SERIES

Each volume in the International Organizations Series is either devoted to one specific organization, or to a number of different organizations operating in a particular region, or engaged in a specific field of activity. The scope of the series is wide-ranging and includes intergovernmental organizations, international non-governmental organizations, and national bodies dealing with international issues. The series is aimed mainly at the English-speaker and each volume provides a selective, annotated, critical bibliography of the organization, or organizations, concerned. The bibliographies cover books, articles, pamphlets, directories, databases and theses and, wherever possible, attention is focused on material about the organizations rather than on the organizations' own publications. Notwithstanding this, the most important official publications, and guides to those publications, will be included. The views expressed in individual volumes, however, are not necessarily those of the publishers.

VOLUMES IN THE SERIES

TITLES IN PREPARATION